RECORDING BRITAIN

RECORDING
BRITAIN

VOLUME III

Lancashire and Westmorland · Derbyshire
Cheshire and Shropshire · Staffordshire
Welsh Counties · Worcestershire
Herefordshire · Oxfordshire
Gloucestershire

EDITED, WITH NOTES, BY
Arnold Palmer

Geoffrey Cumberlege
OXFORD UNIVERSITY PRESS
in association with
THE PILGRIM TRUST
1948

OXFORD UNIVERSITY PRESS
AMEN HOUSE, E.C. 4
London Edinburgh Glasgow New York
Toronto Melbourne Cape Town Bombay
Calcutta Madras Wellington
GEOFFREY CUMBERLEGE
Publisher to the University

PRINTED IN GREAT BRITAIN

CONTENTS

LANCASHIRE AND WESTMORLAND

Askham. *Frances Macdonald* 2

The Ribble at Mitton. *Byron Dawson* 4

Cottage Almshouses, Stydd. *W. Fairclough* . . . 6

Tower Mill, Clifton. *Byron Dawson* 8

Livesey Old Hall, Cherry Tree. *W. Fairclough* . . . 10

White House, near Littleborough. *Albert T. Pile* . . . 12

Hopwood Hall, near Middleton. *Byron Dawson* . . 14

Old Shambles, Manchester. *Albert T. Pile* . . . 16

Ship Canal, Water Street, Manchester. *Albert T. Pile* . . 18

Heaton Hall, Manchester. *Byron Dawson* 20

DERBYSHIRE

Grainfoot Farm, Derwent Dale. *Kenneth Rowntree, A.R.W.S.* . . 24

The Ashopton Inn. *Kenneth Rowntree, A.R.W.S.* . . . 26

Smoke Room, The Ashopton Inn. *Kenneth Rowntree, A.R.W.S.* 28

Underbank Farm, Woodlands, Ashdale. *Kenneth Rowntree, A.R.W.S.* 30

Norton. *Richard Seddon* 32

The Crescent, Buxton. *Kenneth Rowntree, A.R.W.S.* . . 34

Solomon's Temple, Buxton. *Karl Hagedorn* . . . 36

Scarthin Nick. *Norman Webster* 38

St. Mary's, Mappleton. *Malvina Cheek* 40

Ashbourne. *Karl Hagedorn* 42

CHESHIRE AND SHROPSHIRE

Bridge Street, Chester. *Sidney Causer* 46

Row, Watergate Street, Chester. *Sidney Causer* . . . 48

St. Peter's, Chester. *Sidney Causer* 50

Little Moreton Hall. *Barbara Jones* 52

Chapel, Hospital Street, Nantwich. *G. W. Hooper* . . 54

The Rookery, Nantwich. *G. W. Hooper* 56

Milk Street, Shrewsbury. *Edward Walker* 58

23 The Friars, Shrewsbury. *Edward Walker* 60

Stokesay Castle. *Louisa Puller* 62

Broad Street, Ludlow. *E. B. Musman* 64

STAFFORDSHIRE

The Old Hall, Biddulph. *Malvina Cheek* 68

Bethesda, Hanley. *Louisa Puller* 70

The Potteries. *Alan Ian Ronald* 72

Wedgwood Works, Etruria. *Louisa Puller* 74

The Old Vine Inn, Newcastle-under-Lyme. *Michael Rothenstein* . . 76

Almshouses, Newcastle-under-Lyme. *Michael Rothenstein* . . 78

The Round House, Alton. *Barbara Jones* 80

St. Michael's, Stone. *Louisa Puller* 82

Coppice Mill, Stone. *Louisa Puller* 84

Swan Hotel, Stafford. *Michael Rothenstein* 86

Bishop's Palace, Lichfield. *Barbara Jones* 88

WELSH COUNTIES

Toll House, Trewalchmai, Anglesey. *Barbara Jones* . . . 94

Conway Castle and a Coracle. *Kenneth Rowntree, A.R.W.S.* . . 96

Municipal Council Chamber, Bangor. *Kenneth Rowntree, A.R.W.S.* . 98

Addoldy-y-Bedyddwyr, Glyndyfrdwy. *Mildred E. Eldridge, A.R.W.S.* 100

Baptism in the River Ceiriog. *Mildred E. Eldridge, A.R.W.S.* . 102

Garn Dolbenmaen. *R. L. Young* 104

Ddu Allt. *Mona Moore* 106

Chapel, Tremadoc. *Kenneth Rowntree, A.R.W.S.* . . . 108

Wharves, Portmadoc. *Frances Macdonald* 110

Tan-yr-Allt. *Kenneth Rowntree, A.R.W.S.* 112

Peat Cutting, Cefn Coch, Montgomeryshire. *Mildred E. Eldridge,*
A.R.W.S. 114

Pont Dol-y-Moch. *Frances Macdonald* 116

St. Beuno's, Llan-y-Cil. *Frances Macdonald* . . . 118

Slate Fences, Abergynolwyn. *Mildred E. Eldridge, A.R.W.S.* . 120

The Old Parsonage, New Radnor. *Vincent Lines, R.W.S.* . . 122

Laugharne Castle. *Martin Hardie, C.B.E.* . . . 124

Manorbier Castle. *Donald H. Edwards* 126

vi

Old Mill, Clyne Valley. *Mona Moore* 128
Penclawdd, Gower. *Mona Moore* 130
Oystermouth Castle. *Mona Moore* 132
Old Bridge, Bridgend. *Graham Bell* 134

WORCESTERSHIRE

Mill Street Lock, Kidderminster. *Osmond H. Bissell* . . . 138
The Basin, Stourport. *Osmond H. Bissell* 140
Guildhall, Worcester. *Raymond T. Cowern, A.R.W.S.* . . 142
Priory Gateway, Malvern. *Raymond T. Cowern, A.R.W.S.* . 144
The Foley Arms, Malvern. *Raymond T. Cowern, A.R.W.S.* . 146
Woollas Hall, Eckington. *William Grimmond* . . . 148
Upton-on-Severn. *Raymond T. Cowern, A.R.W.S.* . . . 150

HEREFORDSHIRE

Paytoe Hall, Leintwardine. *Louisa Puller* 154
House, Wigmore. *Louisa Puller* 156
Pembridge. *Raymond T. Cowern, A.R.W.S.* 158
Dovecote, Eardisland. *Vincent Lines, R.W.S.* . . . 160
Bosbury. *Raymond T. Cowern, A.R.W.S.* 162
Wye Bridge, Hereford. *Vincent Lines, R.W.S.* . . . 164
Market House, Ledbury. *Raymond T. Cowern, A.R.W.S.* . 166
Market-day, Ledbury. *Raymond T. Cowern, A.R.W.S.* . . 168
Entrance to New Street, Ledbury. *Raymond T. Cowern, A.R.W.S.* . 170
Old Talbot Hotel, Ledbury. *Raymond T. Cowern, A.R.W.S.* . 172

OXFORDSHIRE

Houses by the Bridge, Burford. *Stanley Anderson, R.A.* . . 176
Butter Cross, Witney. *Stanley Anderson, R.A.* . . . 178
Entrance to Botanical Garden, Oxford. *Walter Bayes, R.W.S.* . 180
35 Beaumont Street, Oxford. *Stanley Anderson, R.A.* . . 182
Houses, Thame. *Stanley Anderson, R.A.* 184
The Swan, Tetsworth. *Stanley Anderson, R.A.* . . . 186
White Pond Farm, Stonor. *W. Fairclough* 188
Upper Assenden Farm, Stonor. *W. Fairclough* . . . 190
St. John the Baptist's, Mongewell—East End. *W. Fairclough* . 192

vii

St. John the Baptist's, Mongewell—West End. *W. Fairclough* . . . 194

Bell Street, Henley-on-Thames. *W. Fairclough* 196

Henley Bridge. *W. Fairclough* 198

GLOUCESTERSHIRE

Tithe House, Greet Manor Farm, Winchcomb. *Thomas Hennell, R.W.S.* 202

Music Gallery, Bishop's Cleeve. *A. S. Hartrick, R.W.S.* . . . 204

The Promenade, Cheltenham. *Phyllis Ginger* . . . 206

Montpellier Walk, Cheltenham. *Phyllis Ginger* . . . 208

Thirlestaine House, Cheltenham. *Phyllis Ginger* . . . 210

Painswick. *Stanley Anderson, R.A.* 212

King's Mill House, Painswick. *Michael Rothenstein* . . . 214

Gate-house, Frocester Court. *Robert Swan* 216

Houses, Stroud. *Walter E. Spradbery* 218

The Market, Tetbury. *Louisa Puller* 220

Beverstone Castle, near Tetbury. *Louisa Puller* . . . 222

Double Dovecot, Coln St. Aldwyn. *George Bissill* . . . 224

The Paragon, Clifton. *Phyllis Ginger* 226

ACKNOWLEDGEMENTS

TOO many to name, though they were never too busy to lend their aid, are the custodians and assistants in public and private libraries, in cities and towns, who produced the right volume from among the thousands on their shelves. There are again the rectors, vicars, and curates who sent to inquisitive letters full and patient replies, and were polite enough to seem glad to do so. At different times and places the following ladies and gentlemen have set the editor under the pleasant obligation of thanking them: Mr. Frederick Bowring, Mr. G. Caldecott, Sir William Ll. Davies, Mr. J. Ingman, Mr. Greening Lamborn, Mr. T. C. Macaulay, Mr. J. Nelson Meredith, Mr. C. J. Price, Mr. Cyril Ramsden, Mr. Marshall Sisson, Mr. J. R. Teggin, Professor E. W. Tristram, Miss Elsie M. Verrall, Mrs. Michael Waterhouse, Sir Ralph Wedgwood, Bt., and Dr. Douglas J. B. Wilson.

LANCASHIRE AND WESTMORLAND

Artists

BYRON DAWSON   W. FAIRCLOUGH

FRANCES MACDONALD   E. B. MUSMAN

ALBERT T. PILE

EVEN without a war, Lancashire could scarcely be recorded fast enough. What is left of its landscape is of exceptional beauty, but often it is necessary to shut one's eyes to the chimneys creeping along its valleys and the pylons breaking the line of its crests. As for the towns and cities which, in the industrial areas, form a London-like, an almost uninterrupted mass of brick and stone, they contain little that is not nineteenth century as well as blackish, and that little needs a deal of finding.

Fortunately there are people in the county alive to the situation, and topographical drawing by local artists is encouraged—the most satisfactory method, the method which the Recording Britain collection could not always follow but is designed and, let us hope, destined to stimulate. If, then, as a consequence of local enterprise, only thirty-one drawings of Lancashire were made by only four artists, there are reasons for considering the general position as far better than in certain other counties to which at least twice as much attention was paid. Four of the disappearing windmills of the Fylde district were painted, and seven fine mansions amid the factories in or near Manchester; but good subjects abound in Lancashire as elsewhere, and the artists may be considered to have had, for once, an easier task than the editor. By no other county are the shelves of our public libraries so little bowed.

The light recording of Westmorland and Cumberland was due to other reasons. Neither in war nor in peace are they 'priority' areas; they have been depicted in the works of innumerable artists, native or invading, from De Wint, Glover, and Turner to the art students who, in 1940, were banished by a fatherly Government from South Kensington to Ambleside. It was not until 1943 that Miss Macdonald was asked to make drawings in or near Askham and Haltwhistle.

ASKHAM

Frances Macdonald

Lowther Castle and Lowther River, the stone circles and Askham Hall—for these one must go to Askham; and one might do worse than go there for Ullswater and Haweswater.

Then there is Wordsworth. The poet's father was employed as law-agent by Lord Lonsdale of Lowther Castle, and the poet himself knew the place well (see the sixth book of *The Prelude* and the Dedication to *The Excursion*). To the lovers of the Wordsworths must be added, furthermore, the admirers of the Coleridges, and at times there hovers on the limits of the throng, nervously twisting his cap in his hands, a man who reads Southey.

One way and another, then, Askham has its visitors, if perhaps less numerous than has been made to appear. A.6, or the main road from Glasgow to London, rushing from Carlisle to Kendal and heaving itself over Shap, misses Ullswater, misses the river, the Castle, and the Hall, and misses Askham. People reach the little village by a quieter road from Penrith, crossing from Cumberland to Westmorland by a bridge over the Eamont. This fortunate accident has preserved the character and independence of the place, its cottages, wide street, and village green, so that Askham still looks as it must have looked to the Lake poets.

Francis Frith's ... William Village

THE RIBBLE AT MITTON

Byron Dawson

Two counties have a claim to the picture; but if the view is chiefly of Yorkshire, it is totally from Lancashire. The Ribble at this point belongs to both counties equally, forming the boundary to the large and unexpected encroachment, west and south, made by the West Riding above Clitheroe. Fortunately, this is the only stretch of the frontier which concerns us. Once it leaves the river it is treated, by even the fullest and most reliable works of reference, less with care than with ill-concealed aversion or downright evasion.

Of the works selected from the county group this, perhaps better than any, gives an idea of what all Lancashire must once have looked like. Everywhere there are rivers, often a little smaller than the Ribble but never more delightful; and, near or far, there is always high ground, such as Kemple End here rising behind Mitton Church. Peaceful as the scene is, it was in grave danger when the drawing was done, and may still go the way of the huge area a few miles to the south. There is a plan to erect large chemical works at Mitton.

The church of All Hallows, standing beside the old Manor House, was for a while dedicated to St. Michael and All Angels—not for very long, but since the period happened to be one of activity among gazetteers the saint's name still lingers obstinately in heavy volumes, and adds appreciably to the complexities of the county boundary. The church, a fourteenth-century building (restored 1845), stands in Yorkshire. It contains a number of monuments of the Lancashire family of Shireburns or Sherburnes, whom we shall meet again on the next page.

COTTAGE ALMSHOUSES, STYDD

W. Fairclough

John Shireburn of Bailey was the Duke of Norfolk's agent in Sheffield. A few months before his death, in December 1726, he made a will, instructing his executors 'to build a good almshouse on his estate at Stidd for five poor persons to live separately therein, and to endow it with £30 a year viz. £5 for each inmate and £5 for repairs'.

The manner in which expression was given to his wishes calls loudly for fuller details, and it is tantalizing that they do not seem to be available. Who was the executor, who was the architect, responsible for a building so un-English, and especially so un-Lancastrian, at the end of so modest a lane? What far-away model was smuggled into Ribchester, whence came the inspiration? We are left to make what guesses we can.

Room has been made for a sixth lodging, one on ground level being hidden behind the staircase. The old ladies, members of the Church of Rome, have each a parlour-kitchen, a bedroom, and a larder-scullery. They have also a little money, a little fuel (they prefer to cook on oil stoves), and a garden patch; and they fetch water, as their predecessors have done for two hundred years, from the draw-well just beyond the bottom left corner of the drawing.

Styed Cottages
Mitcheldean   N.E. Angle
                  August 1830.

TOWER MILL, CLIFTON

Byron Dawson

In a district known as the Fylde, east and inland from Blackpool, is a group of wind-mills deserving of more attention than it seems to be receiving. As is the case with most windmills, their condition and prospects are the reverse of satisfactory.

Drawings were made of four of these mills—at Staining, at Little Marton, at Thornton, and, as shown here, at Clifton, six miles from Preston and thus on the southern edge of the area concerned. There is internal evidence suggesting that this large tower mill was constructed or reconstructed in the early years of the eighteenth century, but no details of its history have rewarded a fairly extensive search. The mill was in use until 1935 or thereabouts; the dozen years of idleness have had their effect on the machinery, though the building appears structurally sound. In varying stages of disintegration, four sails remain.

Byron Dawson 1940

LIVESEY OLD HALL, CHERRY TREE

W. Fairclough

Old houses are rare in Blackburn, beautiful ones still rarer; and this, barely two miles from the cotton-weaving centre and hard by the main road to Preston, comes as a surprise. It was built early in the reign of James I and, though repaired or modified twice before the century was out, it has probably kept its original outlines.

Yet, except for survival, the Old Hall has not had much luck. The railway passes within fifty yards of its northern, or farther, side; and before the iron track was laid the house was in decline. At the beginning of the nineteenth century it had come into possession of the Feildens, who destroyed the old garden, formal and walled, but restored the west half of the mansion. That end is still lived in, whereas the other has been allowed to go from bad to worse and become a roofed but hollow shell, a storehouse for chairlegs, wire, and tins, and a shelter for drying linen. Horses, grazing where once the flowers grew, rest their heads on the sills of empty mullions. On the north front, which repeats the arrangement of the southern, the centre projection of the E has collapsed, leaving a gaping hole.

The panel above the first-floor window frames a pious dedication ending with 'ILAL 1608', the initials being ascribed to James and Alice (*née* Bradshaw) Livesey, for whom the house was built. The family first bore the name of Bury; it held the Manor of Livesey for six centuries, and adopted the name of the estate when John was king.

WHITE HOUSE, NEAR LITTLEBOROUGH

Albert T. Pile

The road from Manchester to Halifax has run eleven miles before, on leaving Rochdale, it at last shakes itself free of houses. Then, as it begins the long climb from Littleborough to Blackstone Edge, the views lengthen, the landscape gradually stretches, and the traveller, with a little goodwill in the matter of chimney-stacks along the valleys, can open his eyes.

At the top of Blackstone Edge, 1,250 feet up, stands the White House—the White House Inn when the artist drew it in the autumn of 1942, and now the White House Hotel, though otherwise unchanged. It is not the highest licensed premises in England —that is at Tan Hill, in the North Riding, nearly 500 feet higher—but it is sufficiently bleak. The views are splendid, for the visitors; they are paid for by the staff during severe winters, when the approaches are liable to be impassable for weeks at a time. Defoe and his party, having watched the last of the crops being carted in the valleys on an August afternoon, wandered helplessly along the Edge in a snow blizzard the next morning. He gives three pages to their perils and hardships, and no doubt they were real enough; but every age has its consolations, and for his there was 'the store of good *Ale* which flows plentifully in the most mountainous Part of this Country', and 'the plenty of Coals'.

The road disappearing over the brow of the hill has a very short way to go, barely half a mile, before entering Yorkshire.

HOPWOOD HALL, NEAR MIDDLETON

Byron Dawson

A family taking its name from the place can be traced back to at least the fourteenth century, but the house is a good deal younger—might even be early Jacobean, though it is claimed as Tudor. It is a two-story building of brick and stone, surrounding a quadrangle which in the course of sundry changes has shrunk from its original proportions and lost the large hall on the south side. The changes, indeed, have been rather numerous, but the fine chimneys have survived. In the *Victoria County History* the mansion is described as picturesque rather than architecturally distinguished—a chilly, if just, verdict.

On the Rochdale road, about a mile from Middleton, a modest stone gateway forms the entrance to the long drive. The old house has an agreeable setting of trees, in a scoop on high ground, and is protected by notice-boards—a little strident in the effort to make themselves heard—from the children playing in Hopwood Clough. It has not yet been gripped by the approaching town, but like a good many old country houses, especially in Lancashire, it must be watching, fascinated and unable to move, the waving tentacles.

Capron Dawson 1940

OLD SHAMBLES, MANCHESTER

Albert T. Pile

The street known as Old Shambles must be the shortest in Manchester, and its four houses the oldest. Now that the two end ones, to the right of Ye Olde Wellington Inn, are united as Sinclair's Oyster Rooms, the street is reduced to three premises, unless we include the antique-dealer over Mr. Kenyon's wine shop.

A rather widespread levelling of houses took place in 1720, to make room for the new St. Ann's Square. Old Shambles just escaped then. Two hundred and twenty years later it had a still narrower, a less complete, escape. One side of it is down and has long been carted and swept away; it has ceased to be a passage; and its lurching fronts, once hidden, are now visible from all sides of the new, wide, shapeless expanse spreading unrecognizably between Corporation Street, Victoria Street, Deansgate, Market Street, and Hanging Ditch.

E. KENYON.
Wine & Spirit Merchant
Wine and Spirit

Ye Olde Wellington Inn

Albert T. Pile
Oct. 1902

SHIP CANAL, WATER STREET, MANCHESTER

Albert T. Pile

Farther on in this volume, when we reach Worcestershire, there will be references to the Lancashire canals which, in the eighteenth century, played so large a part in the transformation of the country's communications. The Manchester Ship Canal is of much later date. It was not thought of till 1825; it was not opened till 1894. The passage, obstructed and delayed, of the various Bills through Parliament cost £400,000 in money and, for the Committees, 175 days in time. But the canal brought the sea, thirty-five miles away, to Manchester and made it a major port. The old Bridgewater Canal, joining Manchester to the coal-mines at Worsley and the Mersey at Runcorn, is now owned by the Ship Canal Company.

One brief, almost obliterated, paragraph in the long and complex story may be deciphered in the drawing. From Water Street, just behind the artist's back, a short arm of the canal ran towards the goods-yard of the Central Station, passing beneath the raised building in the middle of the picture. It was used as a dry-dock for barges needing repair; a repairing shed can be seen on the left. For a long time now it has been abandoned and derelict; being officially dry, it served as an air-raid shelter during the war, when the local verdict was 'pretty safe, but wet'. Beyond the lock the canal bed disappears beneath the roadway, and it seems certain that all trace of the old dock is destined to vanish. In the five years that have elapsed since the drawing was made the lock has suffered much from raiders in search of firewood. The lock-keeper's hut owes its survival, no doubt, to the housing shortage.

The high steeple belongs to St. Matthew's, a big church which, like several other churches in Manchester, lost its congregation and was classed as redundant. It awaits demolition; indeed, it is advancing to meet it. Sir Charles Barry designed it in 1825—one of his first essays in Gothic. We are told that he lived to regard it 'as a subject for laughter'.

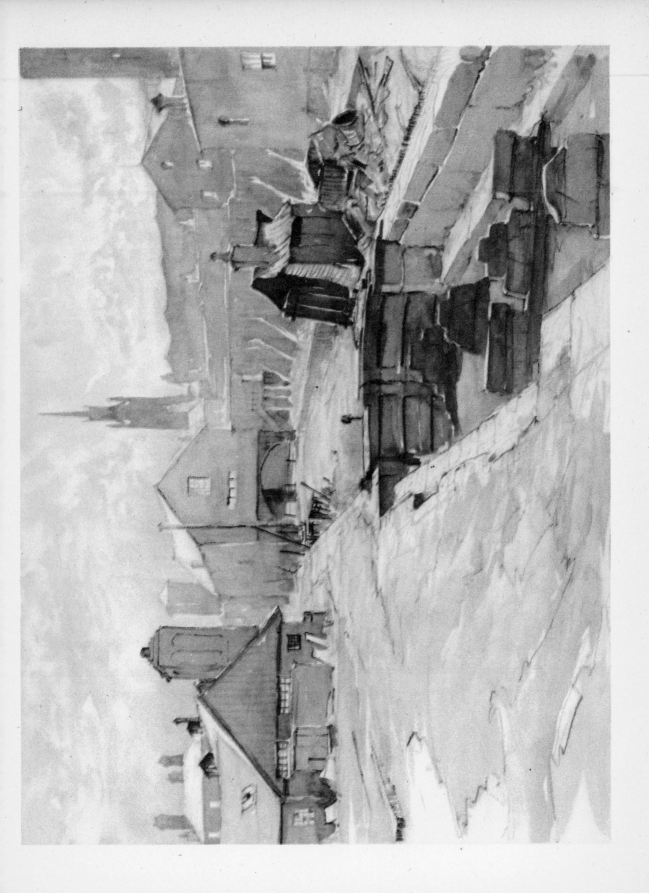

HEATON HALL, MANCHESTER

Byron Dawson

In 1772 James Wyatt refashioned Heaton Hall for Sir Thomas Egerton. The seventh baronet was twenty-three years old; his architect, whose Pantheon had been opened the preceding January, 'amazing' Walpole and ending the ascendancy of Robert Adam, was twenty-six. The Egertons, an old family (the Dukes of Bridgewater were a branch of it), acquired Heaton by marriage, and in the course of a century it had ousted their other estates, in Cheshire, Staffordshire, and Northamptonshire, and become the principal seat.

Wyatt did little to the rather severe northern front, but he entirely changed the southern, breaking it up into bays and recesses, drawing out the centre in a domed projection, and adding wings with colonnaded approaches. The stone façade was ornamented with panelled reliefs and many lovely details; a circular pavilion crowned a rise to the northeast, overlooking the landscaped park and the looping Irwell. Indeed, there was much overlooking. Manchester was still four miles away, and from Wyatt's shapely apartments, wherein his genius for decoration had full scope, the views were of hill and dale and stream. (Visitors should not fail to buy the admirable pamphlet by Mr. Avray Tipping, on sale at the house.)

The 7th baronet became, in 1801, the 1st Earl of Wilton. His grandson and successor, the 2nd Earl, married the daughter of the celebrated actress, Eliza Farren; and her charm, his love of music, and the attraction of their five children all played their part in a long friendship with the Duke of Wellington.

On the lawn facing the saloon windows a large fountain fulfils, on inspection, the promise held out at longer range and commemorates the Diamond Jubilee. It must be almost the last embellishment added by the family before, in 1901, the 5th Earl sold the house and 623 acres of parkland to the Manchester Corporation. The price was £230,000. For very little more much of the contents could have been secured, but the chance was lost. The house is used for the exhibition of pictures overflowing from the City Gallery, the park as a recreation centre. Like Chiswick House, another mansion doctored by Wyatt, Heaton Hall was called up during the war. It has now been demobilized. Wyatt's mantelpieces are still there; some of his ceilings and fanlights, his hall and staircase are there. The view from his windows, however, is not quite there. Broken asphalt paths wander amid huts and hangars, cement blocks, deserted stores, and the split floors of demolished shelters; they conduct the visitor through paper, cartons, bottles, angry notices, chalk-scrawled monuments, orange peel, and overturned litter-baskets to Wyatt's entrance, where stand the sheds of workmen erecting 265 prefabricated houses in a corner of the park. The problem of a stately home has found, at Heaton, what is generally regarded as the ideal solution.

Bryan Dawson 1740

DERBYSHIRE

Artists

MALVINA CHEEK   KARL HAGEDORN
KENNETH ROWNTREE, A.R.W.S.   RICHARD SEDDON
NORMAN WEBSTER

IN no other county was a more precise and urgent task discovered. An application made through the Council for the Preservation of Rural England resulted in a long letter from the local secretary, Mrs. Haythornthwaite, from which two passages are worth quoting. They show what good work the Council is doing through its county branches, and offer a particularly happy illustration of temporary partnership with the Recording Britain Scheme:

'A large and exceptionally beautiful area is now being worked on by the Derwent Valley Water Board for their new Ladybower Reservoir. This is the area round Ashopton and Derwent villages, about twelve miles west of Sheffield. Besides submerging lovely river, woodland, and hill scenery, it will submerge the famous Derwent Hall, Derwent village, and the Packhorse Bridge, which it is hoped to remove and rebuild. Artists' records of this region would be of much historical and aesthetic interest. . . .

'Except for the Derwent region, the area most threatened in our locality is that which was lately taken over from Derbyshire by Sheffield, the scenic attractions of which are as valuable as Derbyshire and form an integral part of it. We would plead that, as the threat to this region is so urgent, it should be included in the artists' records if at all possible. . . . Imminent danger lies in the threat to demolish all rural buildings over 150 years old by our Medical Officer of Health, who considers urban standards (heights of rooms, &c.) should be the same in the country as the town. This means that practically all the stone farms and cottages in the Green Belt, which have their definite local character and charm, are in danger or will be immediately after the War. Areas mainly threatened are the Porter Valley, just west of Sheffield, and the Norton area, south of it. They contain delightful, typical examples, and a record of them would not only be of national interest but might be a great help in our endeavours to get these buildings reconditioned instead of demolished.'

This letter was received during the last days of September 1940. By the following spring Mr. Rowntree had completed a group of sixteen drawings, all but one of them recording land and houses marked for submersion in and around the village of Ashopton. Later, Mr. Seddon supplemented these with eight drawings of the Porter Valley and Norton areas. Mr. Hagedorn had meanwhile done views in Bakewell, where a by-pass project may or may not be dead, and in Dovedale. In all, thirty-two watercolours were painted in the county.

GRAINFOOT FARM, DERWENT DALE

Kenneth Rowntree, A.R.W.S.

The immense reservoir in the Derwent Valley supplies water to Sheffield, Nottingham, and Leicester, as well as to Derby and many Derbyshire towns. It was made in three instalments, between 1899 and 1945, and can produce over 53,000,000 gallons of water every day from the Derwent, the Ashop, and other small rivers and streams fed by the tumultuous slopes of the High Peak district.

At each stage beautiful tracts of country, beloved by holiday-makers from Sheffield and elsewhere, have been submerged; but as the second instalment was completed in 1930, ten years before the Recording Britain Scheme was begun, we are here concerned with the third phase only—the Ladybower reservoir, half as large again as the Howden and the Derwent reservoirs combined.

On the opposite page is the first of four pictures showing what the valleys looked like before being turned into a new Lake District. To-day the scene for many miles has been so unbelievably changed by the vanishing of its floor that precise recognition, or recollection, is impossible without the aid of a photograph, drawing, or painting. The white board on the left is one of many which served (amongst other purposes) to mark the perimeter, thirteen miles in length, of the new reservoir. They also made it possible to estimate whether a building would be sunk, half covered, or left high and comparatively dry. Grainfoot Farm belonged to the second category. Such buildings were usually demolished, but at one point the surface of the lake is still broken by the tall spire of Derwent Church. SS. James and John was rebuilt, and indeed reconsecrated, in 1869, and had limited claims to preservation as a national heritage. Derwent Hall, built in 1672 and pulled down in 1943, was very different. Its oak panelling was extracted and given a new home, also very different—the entrance and Board Room of the Yorkshire Bridge Filter House. As for the small, grey, typical Derbyshire farm-houses, there are, it is true, plenty of them left; but everybody knows the damage done to England, during the last hundred years or so, by that bland and soothing argument.

THE ASHOPTON INN

Kenneth Rowntree, A.R.W.S.

Ashopton, a small place, was well known to excursionists and climbers, and mention of its inn was almost always followed, in the old guide-books, by the words 'well recommended'. It had a name, *The Snake*, but it was customarily called 'The Ashopton Inn' to distinguish it from another *Snake* not far away and even handier for the ascent of Kinderscout.

The inn, the chapel, the Toll Bar House, two farms, and six or seven cottages—the whole village, in fact, as well as the road from Sheffield to Glossop—lie now beneath more than 100 feet of water. A solitary survivor, the seventeenth-century Pack Horse Bridge, was taken down and marked, stone by stone, for re-erection over the River Derwent at Slippery Stones.

Faint in the background on the right of the drawing can be seen the sheer wall of Bamford Edge.

Kenneth Rowntree 40

SMOKE ROOM, THE ASHOPTON INN

Kenneth Rowntree, A.R.W.S.

With its hard benches, iron table, solitary and insufficient ashtray; with its dart-board, stuffed trout, and commercial almanack; with its rubbed wall, courageous wall-paper, and closed window, this corner of the smoke-room was unusually rewarding. Many a man, relying on his early memories and not having used his eyes since leaving the impressionable age, may think this parlour typical enough. It is rapidly ceasing to be so. Even in villages it is being replaced by something shinier; or, awaiting that day, is being smartened up.

Appreciation of how many stories, relief of how many itching bites between the shoulder-blades, rubbed and discoloured that dado? How many good times were had by all? So one might go on; but of all the drawings in the collection this, perhaps, may most confidently be left to speak for itself.

UNDERBANK FARM, WOODLANDS, ASHDALE

Kenneth Rowntree, A.R.W.S.

'The *Woodlands*, a woody glen not surpassed in picturesqueness by any in the county . . . the valley changes in character—it becomes a defile, and the mountain ranges are cleft by deep gorges and advance in precipitous promontories. All the slopes which are not bare rocks are covered with heather and abound in grouse.'

Such was the Woodlands when Murray's *Handbook for Travellers in Derbyshire* appeared in 1874. When, seventy-one years later, the Derwent Valley Water Board issued an illustrated brochure, Murray's view called for certain amendment. 'Bore-holes have been driven into the natural ground at both ends of the embankment and cement grout forced under pressure into any fissures in the strata through which the water might find its way round the ends of the embankment. . . . 100,000 tons of concrete, 1,000,000 tons of earth and 100,000 tons of clay have been used.'

As the white board shows, Underbank Farm just escaped. It still stands; but, with the water lapping so near the front door, no one seems to want it. Agriculturists may be consoled to learn that it had already ceased to be a farm-house and become a week-end cottage. Finally and more generally speaking, it seems fair to conclude this series of regretful notes by recognition that the water boards of England have long been blamed for curtailing supplies in seasons of drought; and that in time to come, when the new bridges and roads have matured and gathered the character that comes with age, the Derwent Valley may be found to have acquired a different, but not necessarily an inferior, beauty.

NORTON

Richard Seddon

Many of the houses and cottages in Norton date from 1600, and are built of millstone grit; it is the prevailing material of the district, and the type of building continued with little change, in south Yorkshire and north Derbyshire, from the fourteenth to the nineteenth century. The style is now abandoned. The seventeenth- and eighteenth-century examples show an occasional classic moulding, and outside stone staircases are fairly common.

For so small a place Norton must be considered to have made a good contribution to the life of the nation. Two members of a local family, the Blyths, achieved bishoprics—Lichfield in 1493 and Salisbury ten years later. A more recent celebrity, commemorated by an obelisk of Cheesewring granite and a monument in the church, is Francis Chantrey (1781–1841) who, having amassed a fortune of £150,000 by the practice of sculpture, founded the well-known bequest which bears his name. He was born and buried at Norton. His father, a carpenter and small farmer, occupied more than one of the houses in his time; Francis's early days were passed in Jordansthorpe which, later, he enlarged for his parents. Here, on the flagstones of the kitchen, Chantrey was allowed to make his first drawings—on Saturdays, just before his mother's weekly scrubbing cleaned the floor again. The milk from his father's farm was sent to Sheffield, four or five miles away, and young Francis carried it.

THE CRESCENT, BUXTON

Kenneth Rowntree, A.R.W.S.

On Friday, 11 June 1790, the Hon. John Byng made this entry in his *Torrington Diaries*: 'Buxton is a most uncomfortable, dreary place; and The Grand Crescent might be better named The Devonshire Infirmary . . . the Duke, I suppose, was made prey of by some architect, a contrast of his Grace, as having some genius, and no fortune.' At this point, surely, the future viscount must have paused and turned the leaf; even after 150 years his sigh of satisfaction is so clearly audible. The Crescent was then new, the sneer was topical, and the diarist saw no need to lose a neat phrase on Truth's vast and empty altar. Yet he must have known very well, of course, that his needy and plausible adventurer was the most famous of northern architects, John Carr of York, then in his 68th year and destined to leave, as his 'no fortune', £150,000.

The 5th Duke of Devonshire, whom we met at Chiswick House, London, had decided that the decayed spa of Buxton should rival Bath, and in 1781 he summoned Carr to outdo the Woods. Bemrose's *Guide to Derbyshire* (1869) talks of 'other resolute and costly efforts', but in fact the Duke's resolve seems to have weakened. The Crescent alone ran him in for £120,000. Later, 'the classic taste of Sir Jeffrey Wyatville and the genius of Sir Joseph Paxton were effectively employed under the stimulative liberality of' the Duke's more dashing successor without, however, seriously troubling the supremacy of Bath.

The Crescent is shorter, stockier, and more deeply concave than most rows of houses bearing the same name. At first view it administers, even, a slight shock. Seldom does opinion change, an unfavourable impression give way to admiration, more quickly and whole-heartedly. In detail as well as in effect, it is a lovely and flawless performance—Carr's masterpiece and more than that, the equal of any comparable construction elsewhere. Unfortunately the site originally chosen was unprocurable, the owner would not sell, and the Crescent was dumped down with its mouth pressed against a dwarfing mound known as St. Anne's Cliff. It cannot be drawn, photographed, or even seen properly; and, to make bad worse, a large stone shelter for St. Anne's Well was added, in 1894, as a further gag to the suffocating Crescent. With Carr's 380 windows, all beautiful, staring them in the face, the owners of the spring have lit the shelter with patterned and coloured glass. . . . Like Mr. Byng, but with a different sort of sigh, we turn the page.

34

SOLOMON'S TEMPLE, BUXTON

Karl Hagedorn

Part curiosity, part monument, Solomon's Temple is a familiar landmark on Grinlow Barrow, two miles south-west of the town. It dates from 1896, but there was another Solomon's Temple there before it; it was built by public subscription to relieve unemployment. No Biblical association coloured its name. The ground belonged to a farmer called Solomon Mycock.

In 1894, just before the erection of the tower, the barrow was opened. Human remains were found. No mention is made of their removal, and possibly they help to support the structure. It is hollow and roofless; by means of an interior staircase one mounts to the battlements, where a magnificent view is obtainable, and a magnificent blow, also.

The road rises gently to Poole's Cavern—an imposing hole, it seems to have thrown the always fretful Defoe into a passion of resentment—and then the climb begins. Guide-books only seventy years old describe the walk as 'easy and frequent', but the congestion is no longer marked, and such sightseers as drag themselves up Diamond Hill are puffing in a manner that would have astonished their grandparents.

SCARTHIN NICK

Norman Webster

Every now and then the Derbyshire scene, always spectacular, writhes into new violence and outdoes itself in stony grimaces. Amidst one of the most famous of these spasms, Matlock occurs; and, of all the approaches to that spa, the road from Cromford on the south is the most romantic and the boldest. Throughout the county there are narrow passes and exiguous valleys where roads, rivers, and railways jostle one another in their flight. The Cromford road, twisting suddenly through a cleft in the rock, is walled in by Scarthin Nick, 200 feet deep, and so conducted to Matlock.

The view, even from the train, is striking. Experienced more closely, it has halted many a painter, set many a poet fingering his lute. James Montgomery (1771–1854) couldn't even wait to get home. While his friend Ebenezer Rhodes, the topographer, surveyed the scene and doubtless, like other topographers, wondered where on earth he should begin, the Sheffield poet drew his style and paid, on the wall of an alcove, his tribute to the landscape and the enduring influence of Pope.

> Here rocks on rocks, on forests forests rise,
> Spurn the low earth and mingle with the skies.
> Great Nature, slumbering by fair Derwent's stream,
> Conceived these giant mountains in a dream.

Portrayed opposite is the beginning of Scarthin Nick. Man. as is his way, has done his best to tame it; some of the teeth seem missing from what Erasmus Darwin called 'old Matlock's marble jaws'; but both cliff and houses are still, for those who know Derbyshire, an epitome.

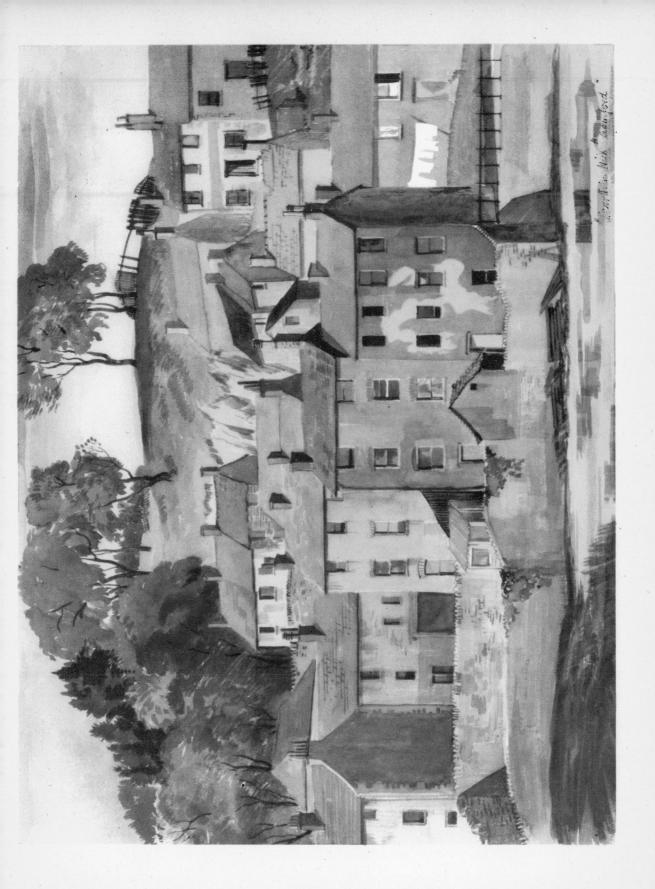

Westgate Mill, Newford.

ST. MARY'S, MAPPLETON

Malvina Cheek

Mappleton (or Mapleton) parish has been consolidated with Ashbourne for eight centuries, but it has a much newer church. St. Mary's was 'thoroughly' repaired, and to a considerable extent rebuilt, about 1850; its size is sufficiently indicated by the cost of that operation, two hundred and fifty pounds. In the graveyard are the normal eighteenth-century tombstones, but from the church itself all plaques and monuments of the earlier building or buildings seem to have disappeared.

It is a very narrow edifice of stone, with a flat wooden roof, and an urn perched surprisingly on its cupola. From the first its appearance excited contempt and even ridicule. Admittedly it has no great claims to beauty and none at all to importance; yet it has lived through its troubles and reached a generation when the formal symmetry of its west front can give mild pleasure, and a picture of it can be painted without any thought of apology or excuse. Miss Cheek's may possibly be the first ever to be made of it since the humble architect laid down his pencil.

Small as it is, the church is big enough for the village. Mappleton is one of those happy places which seem to experience no difficulty in keeping out of the news for a hundred years at a stretch. It is a hundred years since the new St. Mary's shocked the neighbourhood. A hundred years farther back, in 1749, a resident named Mary How, being then 110 years of age, cut a new set of teeth. Two years later, just as life was beginning again at 112, the ever-green widow pulled too eagerly at an apple and broke off, with fatal results, a large limb of the tree.

ASHBOURNE

Karl Hagedorn

More fortunate than Buxton, Ashbourne seems to have had little money spent upon it during the nineteenth century, and it retains a dignity hardly impaired.

No reference to the town can for long avoid the name of Samuel Johnson, and no advantage is gained by delaying the Doctor's entry. His friend, the Rev. Dr. John Taylor, lived here from 1710 to 1788, in a large, red-brick house opposite the sixteenth-century Grammar School, some way down Church Street on the left of the picture. 'Though a schoolfellow and friend of Johnson, he was a Whig', observed Boswell. 'I could not perceive in his character much congeniality of any sort with that of Johnson, who, however, said to me "Sir, he has a very strong understanding".' There was something in Boswell's suggestion; but Johnson paid occasional visits to Taylor over a period of nearly fifty years. He must often have passed this corner and mounted the road to the Square; he must often have seen this tall building, whose bow-windows are to-day incongruously filled with radio apparatus.

The least reflective and most stay-at-home reader of the *Life* will have wondered that the length of the journey was apparently no deterrent. Did the great man remain seated, hour after hour, gazing out at the small, rectangular, grass fields where the limestone rock protrudes through the thin soil, and watching the stone walls change from grey to white beneath the running clouds? Or, on those Derbyshire hills, was he for ever heaving his cumbersome frame on to the road, to ease the coach by walking? We are not told. The rate of express progress can, however, be worked out from Boswell's account of their hurried return to London in 1776 when, on hearing of the death of the Thrales' only son, Harry, they 'whirled' back in a post-chaise. They started 'in the evening', presumably about four o'clock, after dinner. They changed horses at Derby, and slept at Loughborough, having by then covered 30 miles. Of the next day Boswell tells us only that they saw a newspaper at Leicester. (A hundred miles remained; having driven from London to Leicester in the good month of July 1732, Sarah, Duchess of Marlborough, dashed off a note of warning to her granddaughter that 'it is impossible for anybody that is with child to go through such roads without miscarrying'.) Boswell and Johnson did 88 miles the second day, and slept at St. Albans. The whole journey of 140 miles seems to have occupied about 44 hours, of which at least half must have been spent in sleeping, eating, or changing horses. The month was March; the weather drew no comment from the biographer.

CHESHIRE AND SHROPSHIRE

Artists

SIDNEY CAUSER   BARBARA JONES

MALVINA CHEEK   E. B. MUSMAN

G. W. HOOPER   LOUISA PULLER

EDWARD WALKER

LEISURED, expansive, and gentlemanly, the two counties are apt to be envied and linked together, by the rest of the Kingdom, in rosy and well-to-do neighbourliness. This belief, having little or no substantiation, is hard to undermine; nor is this the place to make the attempt since, in the forming of our collection of drawings, the popular view was not contested. Cheshire has its developing areas (round Birkenhead and Crewe), Shropshire has its beauties, rural and urban, but neither county presented notably strong claims for immediate treatment, and neither received it. Unlike the sundial, we toiled in shadow. Fifteen pictures were made in Shropshire and nineteen in Cheshire.

In fact, or at least in landscape, there is sharp divergence between the counties, Shropshire containing almost every known variety of the English scene, Cheshire being on the whole even and uneventful. Nevertheless it is difficult to visit or discuss them without being drawn back to similarities which have their roots in the distant past and still load the air with a common aroma. In the western parts, especially, one can never forget that both are border counties to the once-turbulent Welsh. They are full of the echoes of history from Wales, just as they are rich in half-timbered echoes from Herefordshire in the south. At Chester, Shrewsbury, Ludlow, and Stokesay these echoes swell, reverberate, and drum on the ears, their only fault being, to our prejudiced sense, that they seemed in no danger of diminuendo. Generally, both counties are aware and proud of their heritage, though in the comment of one of the drawings of Shrewsbury a note of uneasiness may be detected.

The eastern, the Derbyshire, Staffordshire, and Worcestershire frontiers have only one representative (Little Moreton Hall) in the pages which follow, but they were not neglected by the recorders. Drawings were made at Stockport, Macclesfield, Sandbach, Mow Cop, Bridgnorth, and Hopton.

BRIDGE STREET, CHESTER

Sidney Causer

Bridge Street, perhaps the widest thoroughfare in Chester, runs down from St. Peter's Church until, at the bottom of the hill, it passes under Joseph Turner's South Gate and over the seven arches of the Old, and red, Dee Bridge. St. Michael's, seen here, is a church of very ancient foundation and modern stone.

For the reader, the main factual interest of the drawing may lie in the balustrades and pillars running above the ground-floor shops on the left of the church. These mark one of Chester's famous Rows—raised arcades approached by staircases. Not only in Bridge Street but in Foregate Street and Watergate Street the almost continuous Rows allow the inhabitants to shop and queue, to hang about or be kept hanging about, in all weathers.

For 500 years distinguished writers have been trying, with limited success, to describe the Rows to readers who have never seen them. William Camden, in his sixteenth-century survey, may be said to have passed the test but hardly to have taken honours. In the seventeenth century the gay and seldom daunted Thomas Fuller girt himself for the task, but soon had to pause, clear his throat, and complain of 'the fashion of them being somewhat hard to conceive'. In the eighteenth century there is Defoe.

'Nor do the Rows as they call them, add any thing, in my Opinion, to the Beauty of the City; but just the contrary, they serve to make the City look both old and ugly: These Rows are certain long Galleries, up one pair of Stairs, which run along the side of the Streets, before all the Houses, tho' joined to them, and as is pretended, they are to keep the People dry in walking along. This they do indeed effectually, but then they take away all the view of the Houses from the Street, nor can a Stranger, that was to ride thro' *Chester*, see any Shops in the City; besides, they make the Shops themselves dark, and the way in them is dark, dirty, and uneven.'

But Defoe was always an irritable traveller. Few hotel-keepers, one imagines, can have been sorry to see him go.

Early in the nineteenth century there appeared George Ormerod's history of Cheshire. His fame is far more restricted than that of the writers already mentioned, but his local knowledge was much greater, and he produced what was then, and is still, the best description.

Sidney Canner. Bridge St. Chester. 1922

ROW, WATERGATE STREET, CHESTER

Sidney Causer

Of the Rows, Ormerod says:

'Their origin appears to be satisfactorily accounted for, in the Vale Royal, on the principle of erecting galleries, from which the citizens might defend themselves against a sudden inroad of armed cavalry. Rows were not however in former days peculiar to Chester. Leland observes of Bridgenorth "There is one very fayre street going from south to north, and on each syde this street the houses be gallered, soe that men may passe dry by them if it raine, according to some streets in Chester cittye".... They form a gallery which occupies the front of the first floor of each house, the buildings over which are supported by columns, and under which are in some instances shops, and in others storehouses and vaults. Some of the latter exhibit specimens of vaulting equal to the cloisters of a Cathedral.'

Accompanying Ormerod's account is a picture of a Row, an engraving of a drawing by George Pickering. It shows two ladies in the costume of the time (1819); except for them, Heath's engraving might have been done from Mr. Causer's drawing, so little has the scene changed. Most of the Rows, it should be explained, are far too full of pedestrians for an artist to be able to stand, sit, or see. The Row shown here, consisting of private dwellings, a small hotel, and the shop of Mr. Aston, a dealer in office furniture, has during school-hours its moments of comparative emptiness and silence. It lacks the beautiful shop fronts still to be noticed on the busier stretches, but seclusion has developed its true character and preserved its echo. Neither Mr. Causer nor George Pickering can have had, for the reason already given, much choice of subject.

Lastly, Henry James, while still a good American, reached and admired Chester and duly tackled the Rows. 'A sort of Gothic edition of the blessed arcades and porticoes of Italy', he called them; '... a flight of steps descends, at frequent intervals, from this superincumbent verandah', and he liked 'the irresistible coquetry of the little shops which adorn these low-browed Rows'. Low-brow had not then its later and now perhaps first meaning. James doubtless wanted to convey the notion of compression, as of a hat pulled down over the eyes.

ST. PETER'S, CHESTER

Sidney Causer

St. Peter's, a building in the prevalent red sandstone, is an unusually square church, a consequence of its site on part of the Roman Praetorium. It has been much changed during the centuries, but still shows Roman work, nearly 2,000 years old, at the base of the pillars. Another curious feature is the colour, red and green, of its painted pews.

Attendance is not easy, for the church stands on narrow and busy cross-roads across which the traffic presses. 'Noticeable as the congestion is to-day, it was', so Mr. Raymond Richards assures us, 'far worse in the centuries that preceded the present one. The high cross standing on a stepped base projected into the street in front of the south door of the church and . . . in the immediate neighbourhood were the pillory, the whipping post, the stocks, and occasionally a gallows. At the angle on the opposite side of the street was the conduit or city water cistern. To add to the congestion at certain times were the crowds attracted by the orations and proclamations delivered from the Pentice, and by the bull and bear baiting which took place at the Cross.' At other times there were tight-rope dancers and mystery-plays. Yet these entertainments were at least stationary; the greater their allurements, the denser the pack in the roadway. The ordeal to-day consists not in the slowness of one's approach but in its extreme rapidity.

Anyone sufficiently resolute and fortunate to reach the sacred precincts will find, with mingled astonishment and relief, a quiet square on the northern side, containing what is said to be the only house of refreshment in positive contact with an English church.

LITTLE MORETON HALL

Barbara Jones

No such house anywhere could fail to be famous; and since it is also starred in Baedeker and safe in the bosom of the National Trust, it is in sharp contrast to those humble, obscure, or precarious affairs which the reader has learned to expect. A number of half-timbered buildings are shown in this volume, especially in Hereford-shire. It is fitting that one of the finest in the country should reveal what the style in full splendour could attain to.

Half-timbered houses arose, for the most part, in districts where local stone was unsuitable or scarce. The importation of stone was, for small houses, economically impracticable; the builders of larger houses might ignore the cost and bring stone from a distance, but Moreton Old (or Little) Hall shows that they did not always do so, preferring to follow to their farthest limits the decorative possibilities of the prevalent style.

There was an earlier mansion; Ormerod, on the evidence of a circular mound within the moat, inferred that it was fortified. The present Hall, which dates from about 1540, was built by, and for a very long time remained in possession of, the Moreton family. We are lucky to have it still. Forty or fifty years ago it was let out in apartments to working-class tenants. A walk round Pimlico will show anyone what, as a rule, is the sequel to that.

Moreton Old Hall

Burne Jones 43

CHAPEL, HOSPITAL STREET, NANTWICH

G. W. Hooper

The Presbyterian Unitarian Chapel (the Rev. Grace Mewhort) stands at the end of a row of cottages set at right angles to the road, and is approached by a paved walk. In all Cheshire there are only eight Nonconformist chapels of sufficient antiquity to qualify for a place in Mr. Raymond Richards's *Old Cheshire Churches*, and this is one of them. The author's note runs as follows:

'Built 1726. It is a small building, but of the traditional form. Its length runs east and west, and the pulpit, formerly in the middle of the south side, was long ago transferred to the north side. The side pews are mounted up in tiers, as in some Calvinist churches on the continent of Europe. The exterior gables have almost a Dutch effect. Here Joseph Priestley, discoverer of oxygen, was minister 1758–61.'

Many earnest people believe that the England of the eighteenth century was an aristocratic enclosure. The career of Priestley might, and perhaps should, make our contemporary social reformers ask themselves in which direction, after all, they are moving. He was the son of a cloth-dresser of Leeds. When he accepted the call to Nantwich he was twenty-five years old, and had already been Presbyterian minister at Needham Market in Suffolk and written *The Scripture Doctrine of Remission*, the first of his many publications. At the age of thirty-three he was elected to Fellowship of the Royal Society, and to the French Academy of Sciences before he was forty. In the intervals of discovering oxygen and the nature of the composition of water he was writing such books as his *History of Early Opinions concerning Jesus Christ*.

The last ten years of his life were spent in America. Supported by the contributions of American and English friends and his own fervent looking for the second coming of Our Lord, the author of *The History and Present State of Electricity* died at Northumberland, Pennsylvania, in 1804. His notice in the *Dictionary of National Biography* fills thirty-nine columns.

THE ROOKERY, NANTWICH

G. W. Hooper

Nantwich holds fine houses of the sixteenth century and later. The Rookery, an early nineteenth-century building, if not among the best of them, might claim to be the unluckiest. Rhododendrons, may, and laburnum in the front garden, clematis beside the porch—they still blossom in due season. But in the flower-beds, beneath the windows, thistles have it all their own way, the window-panes are broken, the side door, not worth locking, swings on its hinges.

It is true that the graciousness of the house is principally external and that the rooms, except the kitchen, are rather small and dark, with the added heaviness of early Victorian decoration. Yet for a long time The Rookery seems to have fulfilled, without difficulty, its role of desirable residence; a member of the Pankhurst family occupied it, and it was favoured by doctors. Perhaps the growing importance of the road junction, outside its gates, destroyed its amenities. Waving half a dozen energetic arms to Crewe, Middlewich, Chester, Stone, the Potteries, Whitchurch, and Audlem, the roundabout might well make a man feel he had no right to stop at his own front door. Clerks of the Urban District Council entered, stayed for a time, then went. Mr. Hooper, as he painted, must have shared the sensations of a man called in to make a death-mask. But The Rookery is not dead. It is to undergo an operation, a series of operations. It may even have its face lifted. It has been bought by a firm of brewers.

The Rushey Mead School 1942

MILK STREET, SHREWSBURY

Edward Walker

Where Belmont approaches Wyle Cop and, in a fit of shyness, changes its name to Milk Street, there stands this Queen Anne corner-house. It is now a tailor's shop, with a ground-level frontage in the latest mode. Next to it, on the side nearer St. Julian's Church, may be seen the bow-window of a dealer in antiques.

This drawing is likely to be of especial interest to future generations. It illustrates a process which is going on everywhere—a process of which the Market Square and many other thoroughfares in Shrewsbury afford striking examples. Mr. George Ward's shop of antiques dates, in its present form, from the reign of James I. Its curving window is a later addition made, very possibly, when the larger house was being built, and is therefore an anachronism. In the course of time, however, the shop has acquired harmony and will, one may reasonably hope, be respected. About the architectural future of Mr. Shields's tailoring establishment there is far less room for optimism. Clearly, the building was once a fine, commodious, town residence—indeed, it has kept its beautiful brow, eyes, and nose, so to speak, but it has lost its mouth and chin, its front door and ground-floor windows. Some day, near or far, the business will change, the premises fall vacant, and no one can say for what purpose the place may be acquired. But since the twentieth-century shop is never likely to learn eighteenth-century ways, since the house has already been grievously damaged, since enterprise should not be checked, since the world must go on—for a dozen convincing reasons any plea for the retention of the upper stories can be and will be made to look like obstructive sentimentality.

In every town in England you can see, if you care to raise your eyes, beautiful tops to ugly shops; and you can know, if you care to think, that the next stage is not the righting of a wrong but just the opposite—the obliteration of the last, silent, reproachful, doubt-engendering, admiration-stealing traces of it.

MILK STREET SHREWSBURY   Edward Walker 6 Oct 1943

23 THE FRIARS, SHREWSBURY

Edward Walker

Near the English Bridge, the crossing of the Severn east of the 'island', are a few remains of the Grey, or Franciscan, Friary. They help now to form a courtyard of little houses, with traces of origin most clearly revealed in No. 23 and especially in its doorway. The familiar pinkish stone of which the houses are constructed was laid in the thirteenth or fourteenth century, at a time when there were barely a dozen stone houses in Shrewsbury. The Friary was, in fact, outside the first, or Norman, wall, but within the later wall erected about 1250. These houses are certainly less than a hundred years younger than the second wall. For further details, the reader should turn to *The Old Houses of Shrewsbury*, by H. E. Forrest.

The usual tunnel runs beneath No. 23; it has, as usual, been blocked up; and there is the usual doubt as to its course and exit. Residents in The Friars can be persuaded to suggest, with an almost visible shudder, that it was dug to facilitate infiltration from the Roman Catholic Cathedral designed by the younger Pugin in 1856.

Nº 23 THE FRIARS, SHREWSBURY   Edward Walker 28ᵗʰ Oct. 1943

STOKESAY CASTLE

Louisa Puller

The art of constructing great castles, with the baron and his army of retainers accommodated within impregnable stone walls, was at its zenith in the twelfth century. A change was inevitable. To sit all day in a windowless drill hall, coughing and weeping in the smoke of a huge bonfire and half a hundred torches, may have been good enough for the baron's father and mother; a day was bound to come when it would no longer be good enough for his wife. Stories of clever new inventions, called fire-places, chimneys, glass, were reaching her ears; we can imagine that she mentioned them to the baron, and even dwelt upon them. The fortified manor arrived. It still had walls and a moat, and a tower into which the inmates retired when attacked. But it was principally, if primitively, a residence, the country-house in embryo; and if, when danger drove the owners out of their house and into their tower, the dwelling-quarters were sometimes burned by the assailants, the house would be rebuilt and, no doubt, a few more comforts included. Unnoticed at the time, and still apt to be overlooked by feminists, the domestic balance was gradually but firmly shifted. Great ladies had been responsible for the hopeless task of making castles comfortable. Now they began to have houses which their husbands were expected to defend.

As private feuds dwindled, the towers might be either allowed to fall into decay or pulled down to furnish material for additions to the house. Most of the fortified manors which survived to the seventeenth century met their end in the Civil War. Of the few remaining, Stokesay is the best, as well as the oldest, example. We owe its preservation to the prudence of its garrison who, having watched Cromwell's men mounting their cannon and heard two bullets strike the door, surrendered.

Stokesay was built in the thirteenth century and fortified after building; it is not far from the Welsh border. Its moat is sufficiently wide to be laid out to-day as a fruit and vegetable garden. Several drawings were made. The one here reproduced shows in the distance on the left, across the once walled courtyard, the Elizabethan gateway, and as its main subject the north end of the Hall, where the tall windows are notable specimens of early domestic architecture. The half-timbered exterior of the upper room is, of course, a much later addition, but the room itself is an original and important feature. The entire family lived and slept in it. The tower can be seen rising above the far end of the Hall.

BROAD STREET, LUDLOW

E. B. Musman

For its size, Ludlow receives from the compilers of guide-books as much attention as any town in England. Every tourist, at least every American tourist, knows it; it is so famous, and has been so often recorded by artist and photographer, that it had no strong claims for inclusion in the present collection. But though the Norman and storied castle, the great church, and the elaborate half-timbered houses are all duly and dutifully commemorated, the whole is apt to be obscured by the parts. Only occasionally, by writers like Mr. Christopher Hussey, is the architectural sequence noted and emphasized.

Here, looking up Broad Street from the only survivor of the town's seven gates, seventeenth- and eighteenth-century fronts, sandstone and brick, mingle without any embarrassment with the black and white houses at the top. The loneliness of the two mid-Victorian structures, facing one another in the middle of the street, is the sole interruption to the general congeniality.

The short walk is rewarding, and all the time one is approaching the beautiful building at the end—the Butter Cross erected in 1743-4 to the design of William Baker. He was a local man, a farmer as well as an architect; not much seems to be known about him and, for that very reason, the mere mention of his name affords pleasure. Provincial England is still full of the work of such men, their names, even if they can be discovered, often half-forgotten. Everyone has heard of the Woods of Bath; many are familiar with the name of Carr of York and (not so many) with that of John Abel of Herefordshire. But very few people outside their locality have even heard of Henry Bell of Lynn, William Hayward of Shrewsbury, Henry Briant of Reading, R. H. Sharp of York, Thomas White of Worcester, John Johnson of Chelmsford, John Harvey at Stafford, or Joseph Turner on the North Wales border. Dozens might be added. They lived in the refulgent days of their profession, and the humblest of them could not altogether escape the glow.

STAFFORDSHIRE

Artists

MALVINA CHEEK   BARBARA JONES

LOUISA PULLER   ALAN IAN RONALD

MICHAEL ROTHENSTEIN

IN many county galleries and libraries one may see topographical drawings and engravings. Recording is unceasing, if usually haphazard. We live in an age of great and swift changes; it is the moment for private benefactors or public or semi-public authorities to commission, buy, or borrow more drawings and, in particular, to decide what the subjects of those drawings should be. By handing on a picture of their county as they know it, they will give satisfaction to themselves, educate their generation, and delight its successors.

If such hopes, held for every county, are mentioned here, that is because Staffordshire, with its striking contrasts, lends itself to analysis and purposeful recording. Clear objectives abound. There is the 'Black Country', a term often misapplied but belonging strictly to the South Staffordshire coalfields and Wolverhampton. Very different, much smaller and more compact, but yet a counterpoise in the northern half of the county, are the Potteries. Between and around these industrial areas stretches, wonderfully beautiful, a varying country-side—moorland in the north, a Rhineland at Alton, agricultural land everywhere—the inhabitants of which are still apt to be unfamiliar with places and people outside their immediate surroundings. The eastern frontier of Dovedale shares the stoniness of Derbyshire; over the flatter western border spill the half-timbered houses of Shropshire and Cheshire. The Georgian streets and houses of the centre form another contrast with the dark-brown stone and tiles of the north; and there are the old farm-houses with details all their own. All these features are being modified slowly or disappearing steadily, as suburban villas spread, as old houses are replaced by new, as industrial methods change.

This brief account of one of the loveliest counties gives some idea of what is meant by planned recording, of what is wanted. An attempt was made to include examples of the more characteristic features but, as usual, the goal seemed to recede faster than the attackers could advance. In particular, and with regret, the farm-houses had to be almost entirely ignored. The thirty-two drawings in the group represent a very tiny fragment of what calls for recording in Staffordshire.

THE OLD HALL, BIDDULPH

Malvina Cheek

When built by Francis Biddulph in the year of the Armada, the Hall was a fine, and no doubt a fortified, Elizabethan manor-house, in the dark-brown stone and tiles peculiar to the moorland country. It lasted only fifty-five years. His grandson was an active and devoted adherent of King Charles, and in 1643 his home was besieged, and finally destroyed. As yet another proof, if another be needed, that the divisions of the Civil War were vertical as well as horizontal, splitting families no less than classes, it may be noted that the assailants were led by Sir William Brereton, while the defenders were under the command of his nephew, Lord Brereton. The Breretons were great people in the district, and many an honest fellow, puzzled by the clamour and arguments of the warring parties, must have wished that they would make up their minds, and his.

High up on the edge of Congleton Ridge, invisible amongst trees, the Hall proved as difficult to attack as it now is to find. A big gun known as 'Roaring Meg' had to be dragged over 25 or 30 miles of seventeenth-century roads, all the way from Stafford to the borders of Cheshire and Derbyshire, before the house was captured. How thoroughly Sir William did his job can still be seen three hundred years later. One end of the Hall has been rebuilt and is a farm-house. The rest, three sides of a roofless rectangle of openwork brick walls, now serves as a frame round a lawn fringed with flowers.

BETHESDA, HANLEY

Louisa Puller

Meetings which grew too big for sitting-rooms and then for coach-houses led to the erection, in 1798, of a Methodist Chapel in Albion Street, capable of seating 600. John and Charles Wesley had both died within the preceding decade, but it was clear that nothing now could check the momentum of the movement they had started. Thirteen years later the Trustees decided to increase the seating capacity to 1,000; and after another eight years, in 1819, the original chapel was pulled down, being again outgrown. By 1824 the congregation had the existing chapel, holding 2,000; they also had a debt of £7,000, which they bravely discharged. Like Inigo Jones, the designer of the Bethesda was 'not exactly what one would call an architect'. He was Mr. Perkins, a schoolmaster.

It is not a beautiful building, but it is spacious, well planned, and admirably kept. The utter desolation of the surrounding cemetery, where in summer the weeds top the tombstones, provides not only a marked contrast but even something of a shock. The aspect, magisterial and subfusc, of the Corinthian front in Albion Street gives no hint of what lies behind.

THE POTTERIES

Alan Ian Ronald

Stoke, Hanley, Burslem, Tunstall, and Longton (Baedeker adds Fenton) are 'unique and indispensable. . . . They are unique and indispensable because you cannot drink tea out of a teacup without the aid of the Five Towns; because you cannot eat a meal in decency without the aid of the Five Towns. For this the architecture of the Five Towns is an architecture of ovens and chimneys; for this its atmosphere is as black as its mud . . . for this it is unlearned in the ways of agriculture, never having seen corn except as packing straw and in quartern loaves; for this it lives crammed together in slippery streets where the housewife must change white window-curtains at least once a fortnight . . . for this it gets up in the mass at six a.m., winter and summer . . . for this it exists— that you may drink tea out of a teacup and toy with a chop on a plate. All the everyday crockery used in the kingdom is made in the Five Towns—all, and much besides. . . . Wherever in all England a woman washes up, she washes up the product of the district.'

To go on quoting from *The Old Wives' Tale* would be more than easy; it would be highly congenial. But though Bennett's descriptions are unlikely to be bettered they and this drawing may both become, in time, period pieces.

The writer of the following comment is as native to the scene as Bennett; forty years separate the two utterances.

'In the industrial district of the Potteries it is the shape and appearance of the Pot Works themselves that is most characteristic and can be called grotesque or picturesque as you choose to look at it. The Works consist mainly of groups of kilns, anything up to a dozen in a group, each kiln looking like a huge, flat-bottomed water bottle. . . . It would be heresy to say so in North Staffordshire, but I venture to think that the kilns may properly be regarded as part of Vanishing England. I feel sure that they will disappear in the next thirty years and be succeeded by "tunnel ovens", more economical but not half so queer.'

In the preface which he wrote for the 1911 edition of his book Bennett talks of 'change . . . made up of an infinite number of infinitesimal changes, each unperceived'. He was alluding to the woman whose appearance, in a restaurant in the Rue de Clichy, was the starting-point of his novel; but his words, having a universal application, are just as well suited to the ultimate setting of the story.

WEDGWOOD WORKS, ETRURIA

Louisa Puller

In 1766 Josiah Wedgwood the first, being then 36 years of age and recently wedded to his cousin, bought the Ridge House Estate, between Hanley and Newcastle, for £3,000. Here he built a house for himself and a new factory, giving to them both (in salutation of the old Etruscan pottery) the name of Etruria. The factory was opened in 1769, and confined at first to ornamental ware, the production of 'useful' ware being left at his old Bell Works at Burslem. After four years the Burslem establishment was closed and all production concentrated at Etruria.

Meanwhile the Duke of Bridgewater and James Brindley, that famous pair whom we shall be meeting again in Worcestershire, had already begun, in 1764, the parliamentary and engineering preliminaries of the Trent and Mersey Canal. Wedgwood, who, like all manufacturers of perishable or fragile goods, was constantly impeded by the state of the roads, subscribed £1,000 towards the cost and became the honorary treasurer of the scheme; and when eventually, in 1777, five years after Brindley's death, the canal was completed, it passed through the Etruria estate, with a branch running right down to the works. Freight charges fell from 10d. to 1$\frac{3}{4}d$. per ton per mile. In time—that is to say, in the course of 160 or 170 years—the Etruria works subsided, as a result of mining operations, well below the level of the canal; and for this and other reasons the manufacture of Wedgwood ware has now been almost entirely transferred to the new factory at Barlaston. But the canal 'is still the chief means of transporting clays and flints from Runcorn, near Liverpool, whither they have been conveyed by sea from Devon and Cornwall and the north coast of France'; and there is still a corner of Etruria, shown in the picture, where certain activities linger, awaiting removal to their new quarters. The open door in the centre admits to No. 1 oven, with the furnace-men's eating-house and the cup-handlers' and turners' room on the right, the china biscuit warehouse up the curving stairs to the left and, more to the side, the casting shop.

Over the ground where Miss Puller took up her position there have passed, during the years and in the service of the firm, other members of her profession—John Flaxman, George Stubbs, Eric Ravilious, and an illustrator of early catalogues, William Blake.

THE OLD VINE INN, NEWCASTLE-UNDER-LYME

Michael Rothenstein

The name has a local vogue. Old Vine Inns are to be seen at Nantwich, Stafford, and other places, and they seem always to be old and occasionally to be vine-clad.

In the house on Bridge Street (landlord, Mr. Barber) there are features to distress the aesthetes and to delight those more robust fellows, the artists. The front door and the wooden surrounds of the windows are painted a shining khaki. The pediment over the door is a mat chocolate, and rests on pillars papered in rosy marble. The bar windows are variegated with stained glass.

All this, as may be imagined, makes a happy symphony. Since the drawing was done, however, the old house has undergone a change which will be deplored by artists and aesthetes alike, by everybody except the uneducated and ruthless people responsible for it. The title of the inn has been painted, in a style of already outmoded modernity, between the two left windows of the first floor; the beautiful and well-spaced lettering above the door has been erased; and the now blank panel occupied by a swinging sign repeating once again the brewers' name. Business, it must never be forgotten, is business. Yet if the thirsty, looking down the street, were apt to be unaware of the existence of *The Old Vine* and to take their custom elsewhere, the panel might still have been respected and the swinging sign placed just as effectively between the two windows. The loss of character in the appearance of the house is very great; and though it may be thought, generally speaking, to be a matter of the slightest consequence, such little things, done everywhere and every day, add up and multiply. There is a whole sermon in this drawing of a small pub in a small street.

ALMSHOUSES, NEWCASTLE-UNDER-LYME

Michael Rothenstein

Delayed action, conflicting dates, multiplied benefits, noble but unexpected names on almost illegible tablets—all are present to complicate the story of the almshouses. It would be difficult—or, as more practised writers say, tedious—to trace the details in full and allocate the credit. Fortunately, there is no doubt concerning the Founder. He was Christopher, 2nd Duke of Albemarle, a considerable man overshadowed by a more than considerable father. He was the only son of the 1st Duke, better known as George Monk or Monck, the wary Cromwellian general who, though perhaps the chief agent in placing Charles II on the throne, sticks in most people's minds as the father of the Coldstream Guards.

The foundation of the almshouses dates from 1687. In the November of that year the Duke, who, as Chancellor of the University of Cambridge, had had to resist papist and political mandates of King James, was appointed Governor of Jamaica. He died there a few months later.

The fund, which made provision not only for the housing of twenty poor widows but also for a weekly allowance of three shillings apiece (four shillings at Christmas), was not translated into the present building, on Upper Green, until 1743. Possibly the almshouses, when new, may have had a somewhat institutional air; if so, the passage of two hundred years has softened it into a serene dignity.

Moorside. St Paul's Town. 1943.

THE ROUND HOUSE, ALTON

Barbara Jones

Guide-books are fond of alluding to Alton as 'the Rhineland of England'. It is an apt phrase, giving with brevity and vividness the character of the abrupt, startling scene. True, the Churnet is not the Rhine; on its pinched bosom lie no steamers with black and white funnels, scents of *Mittagsessen*, and blasts of Wagner. But the wooded steeps are there, and so are the gaudy castellations crowning them; and they are part of the story of the lock-up away in the village street across the valley.

In 1814 John Talbot, 15th Earl of Shrewsbury, conceived the idea of amassing 'an extensive pile of Gothic masonry' to overlook the Gothic landscape. Panelled, stained-glassed, dim and jumbled, it painfully arose; and down from it the valley was filled with fountains, arcades, a coroneted conservatory, a pagoda, a tower, a flag-turret, rusticated bridges, and other assorted monuments, to which was added a Choragic temple sheltering a bust of the earl inscribed 'He made the Desert smile'. Many features were built, pulled down, and refashioned nearer to the earl's desire. He was, as Pitt observed, 'somewhat fanciful'. Employing local architects for the premises, he summoned Brown for the park. Every kind of exotic tree and shrub, somehow accommodated, went to form a second Kew, and then (presumably when Brown's back was turned) more and more trees were planted until every vista was blocked, every grot, urn, statue, column, hermitage, ruin, and pavilion was hidden from sight and invested with ever-dwindling surprise. At any time, too, herds of wild cattle, grey as doves and ferocious as rhinoceri, might diversify the glades, give point to a stroll, and add to the attraction of the temples. Such was, such largely is, Alton Towers. Irresistibly, inevitably, it attracted to itself the right, the ideally florid pen. As Muriel Towers, 'the chief seat of his race', it is the setting for the hero of *Lothair*.

The 15th Earl, dying in 1827, did not live to see his vision realized; the 16th, without disturbing, slipped into the dream and even extended it. He called Pugin to his aid, and one would gladly attribute the lock-up to him, but it seems to have been constructed before his arrival. In language at once ambiguous and clear, the county *Gazetteer & Directory* for 1834 states that 'A *Round-house* or lock-up, for securing prisoners, has lately been erected by the Earl of Shrewsbury, whose other seats are at Heythorpe House, Oxfordshire, and Grafton Hall, Worcestershire'. Lock-ups were already falling into disuse; and this one—spacious and, with its rings of stone bolsters, even decorative—was used for only fifteen years. Then the Earl, impractical perhaps but never small-minded or unreceptive of new ideas, presented Alton with a police-station.

Adam Lock-up. Staffs. Barbara Jones 1943

ST. MICHAEL'S, STONE

Louisa Puller

The new factory at Barlaston, well built, handsome, a model of its kind, is none the less a factory; and some of the older and more apprehensive residents of Stone may reflect that the Potteries, which used to be seven miles away, have now a representative at under a league.

The pleasant town seems, therefore, fit for the attention of local artists, to supplement the four or five drawings made by Miss Puller. Here is one of them—the parish church of St. Michael, surrounded by its garden-wall, on rising ground at the south end of Stone. It is not an old building, being the successor to a church which fell down in 1749, but it has some fine memorials and graves. Several of these commemorate the (Jervis) family of that great sailor, the 1st Lord St. Vincent, born and buried at Stone; one, a large mural tablet near the west door, is notable for an obituary of astonishing pomposity and wordiness. It runs to some ninety lines, and must deserve a place among the longest eulogies that ever began by amusing, and ended by boring, a chiseller.

COPPICE MILL, STONE

Louisa Puller

The water-mill tucked away in a dell three parts of a mile from Stone, on the Longton road, is one of six little mills beside the Moddershall stream. In spite of their rural surroundings they are an offshoot of the smoke-laden towns of Hanley, Burslem, and Stoke, six miles away. They are entirely dependent on the Potteries, and workers in the Potteries who have never seen or heard of them and take not the faintest interest in them are partly dependent on their products. These mills do not grind cereals; they grind the most important constituent of earthenware, flint. Flint 'reduces the contraction of the body, enabling it to be fried at a higher temperature without cracking or losing shape and yet retaining sufficient porosity to take a coating of glaze. It adds to the whiteness of the ware. A body without flint would almost certainly craze badly (i.e. the glaze would have a network of fine cracks) and be useless for table or sanitary purposes.'

All the raw materials of the Potteries have to be brought from elsewhere—china-clay from Cornwall, ball clay from Dorset, felspar from Derbyshire, with a brisk trade in bones from South America. The flint pebbles, which at one time were drawn from Norfolk, Sussex, and the coast of Normandy, more often come now from Kent. After being cracked and shattered they are fed to the grinding-pan, consisting of a hard stone (chert) base. Over this revolve two or more heavy blocks of chert (silica) stone, weighing two or three tons. Water is added with the charge, and the grinding takes at least twelve hours. The product, in the form of a thick white 'liquid', is generally dried on the spot before being transported.

The process of 'pan' grinding is slowly being replaced by cylinder grinding, more easily controlled and more economical of power. Most of the great pottery works have, in fact, long possessed their own grinding machinery. Presumably, when these mills were started, water-power was still cheaper than coal, and the flint millers found in the Moddershall a convenient source of profit. Coppice Mill, like its fellows, cannot be much more than 100 years old. Mr. Shardlow's flint all goes into sanitary ware—baths, basins, pans, for hotels, railway stations, offices, flats, and houses.

SWAN HOTEL, STAFFORD

Michael Rothenstein

A few steps south of the Shire Hall (a very satisfying work by John Harvey, 1794) Greengate Street leads to the *Swan Hotel*. Many of its visible features suggest the time of George I; what is hidden is doubtless much older and may well have been an outlying building of the adjoining church of St. Mary's.

However fragmentary, varied, and obscure its earlier history, its condition in 1825 has been described at some length by George Borrow in *The Romany Rye* (chs. 23–9). He arrived there with a fine horse which he had bought cheaply with Jasper Petulengro's money, and at once, as was his habit, made friends with a postilion. Through the postilion, Borrow met the landlord and was immediately engaged—or, as he would prefer us to think, allowed himself to be engaged—as 'general superintendent of the yard' and keeper of the hay and corn bills. After working off a joke about the landlord's distinguished appearance (an old and exhausted joke, even then) he settles down to describe the arrangement and custom of the inn. It was, of course, a coaching inn. There was an archway, possibly between the two bow-windows where the front door now stands, and coaches drove into a yard crowded with public and private vehicles and swarming with ostlers, postilions, coachmen, grooms, potboys, boots, and stray people who had long talks with Borrow. Besides the waiters, chambermaids, cooks, and scullions, employed indoors were three shoe-blacks and a hairdresser. 'A vast number of sporting people' frequented the house, 'the first road-house in England'. The cellar was particularly choice.

Borrow, twenty-two and without means, threw up the job after a week or so and, ignoring the advice of Francis Ardry, the gold of the landlord, and the affectionate remonstrances of the staff, rode off for Horncastle horse-fair. It is part of his charm, perhaps the part that draws us back to him again and again, that we can never entirely believe or disbelieve him; but there is no reason to suspect his description of the *Swan*.

SWAN HOTEL

SWAN HOTEL

Michael Rothenstein · 1943.

BISHOP'S PALACE, LICHFIELD

Barbara Jones

The Bishop's Palace, of which the south or garden side is here shown, was built in 1687. It is one of several splendid houses which, in or adjoining the Close, are apt to divert the attention of the Cathedral visitors. The nineteenth-century Dean who, whenever invited to dinner, would arrive from his lovely Deanery next door 'drawn in his carriage and pair of greys' showed that he understood what was due to Palace as well as to Bishop.

It is no disparagement of Their Lordships, an illustrious succession, to say that many of the most distinguished callers at the Palace have not been in search of a bishop. During the second half of the eighteenth century a Canon was in residence. Author of a sermon entitled *The late dreadful Earthquakes no proof of God's particular Wrath against the Portuguese*, Canon Seward won even wider recognition as the father of a poet; and after his death in 1790 his daughter Anna continued to reside and hold literary court in the Palace for the remainder of her life, another nineteen years. She lived in, she presided over, an age of poetesses. Seldom has such renown vanished so utterly. Long before Quiller-Couch ignored her, Mrs. Valentine's *Gems of National Poetry* had glittered without her light; why, she had petered out by Palgrave. As early as 1844 that more-than-anthologist, Robert Chambers, had only just found room for her in his *Cyclopaedia of English Literature*. Muttering something about a 'tuneful sisterhood' he crammed her, with four other song-stresses, into a bare half-page.

'Before she was nine years of age, she could repeat the three first books of Paradise Lost. . . . Miss Seward wrote several elegiac poems which enjoyed great celebrity . . . and she was known by the name of the Swan of Lichfield . . . Miss Seward engaged Sir Walter Scott in a literary correspondence, and bequeathed to him for publication three volumes of her poetry, which he pronounced execrable. . . . Her publisher gave to the world six volumes of her letters. Both collections were unsuccessful.'

Even in her lifetime there were those who could not wait for the Swan's dying notes. Walpole classed her with 'half-a-dozen of those harmonious virgins' whose 'thoughts and phrases are like their gowns, old remnants cut and turned'. Yet the best opinion was against him and for her. Scott wrote the lines on her tomb; Leigh Hunt praised her; Romney painted her; Southey, Hayley, Thomas Day, Erasmus Darwin, and Mrs. Thrale were glad to be counted among her friends. Boswell spoke of her with the greatest respect, and Johnson (whom she abominated) declared some of her work to be matchless. She cannot have a single reader left. There is something here we do not now understand.

Barbara Jones 1943

Bishop's Palace Lichfield. 687

WELSH COUNTIES

Artists

GRAHAM BELL	A. M. HIND
OLIVE COOK	BARBARA JONES
H. E. DU PLESSIS	VINCENT LINES, R.W.S.
DONALD H. EDWARDS	FRANCES MACDONALD
MILDRED E. ELDRIDGE	MONA MOORE
MARTIN HARDIE, C.B.E.	KENNETH ROWNTREE, A.R.W.S.

R. L. YOUNG

MAN'S ingenuity and constant pressure are much more easily forgotten in Wales than in England. If the recording of Wales had been limited to areas changed, or being changed, by exploitation, a very unrepresentative, a semi-anglicized, group consisting principally of Glamorganshire and the Rhyl–Llandudno coast would have ensued; for such areas are confined, in the main, to the surroundings of the coal-mines, the harbours, the watering-places, and (less positively) the slate quarries, and there are whole counties which contain none of these. Whole counties (Brecon and Cardigan) were, in fact, left unvisited. Wales was treated as a whole, and its wild scenery, its musical streams, its stone cottages, and other features of the quiet inland were recorded wherever suitable and convenient. A Welshman would find it hard to place, unaided, many of these drawings done by the wayside.

Nevertheless the purpose of the scheme was kept in mind, and more pictures were painted in Glamorganshire than in any other county. Merioneth, with its slate quarries and its unsurpassed landscape, came second, followed by its rival and neighbour, Caernarvonshire.

Besides the scenery and the buildings, much else that is evocative of the ancient and separate life of the Principality called for notice. Farm wagons and sleigh wagons, river boats, costume, chapels, peat-digging, slate fences and slate tombstones as well as the quarries themselves, summer dairy houses high on the mountain slopes, open-air baptism by immersion, an eisteddfod—these with a few castles which, though not now drawn for the first time, were needed as a growling bass, are some of the specialities recorded for future generations. Many of them could hardly have been procured from a foreigner; they are due to the knowledge, skill, and enthusiasm of a resident artist, Mildred Eldridge.

Much persistence was called for from the artists, and behind their pictures the idle reader should often make for himself another picture of a bicycle, a mountain road, and a snowy wind. They may have been helped by the constant and surrounding signs of similar persistence displayed in a form not always suited to the brush. The names of Welshmen seem, to a certain type of Englishman, a joke of which he never tires; and indeed we may as well admit that most visitors, and some natives, find in the sight of four or five shops in a row, each owned by a different Evans, something comical. But there is another aspect of the matter, revealed nowhere more strikingly than in graveyard after graveyard of the chapels and churches. Rhys, Price, Hughes, Evans, Owen, Jones, Lloyd, Davies, Williams, Morgan, Llewellyn, Roberts, Watkins, Griffith, Morris, Howell, Wynne, Thomas, Ellis, Jenkins, Vaughan, Parry, Lewis—these names recur again and again, nor do they merely recur, twenty or thirty names which hardly vary, which almost exclude all others. There is nothing comical in a national life like that, in such evidences of persistence, resistance; and nothing surprising in the bearers of those names speaking a language of their own. The number of Welsh children who have to be taught English when first they go to school, the number of adult Welsh who continue to speak their own tongue, reserving their use of English for business purposes or the reading of English books and newspapers, is in approximate proportion fifteen times greater than the equivalent figure for Scotland and fifty per cent. higher than the equivalent figure for Eire, in spite of the Irish Sea, St. George's Channel, Lady Gregory, and the edicts of Dail Eireann. Not enough, not nearly enough, attention has been paid to the Welsh character. Not the least of the virtues of the next twenty-one pictures is the provision of traces of this character.

Like all distinct flavours, it does not make a universal appeal, and there are parallels between it and the not always acquired taste of those two English writers who, at the mention of Wales in a literary assembly, are apt to come first into the mind and the conversation. One sought the bypaths, talking and walking with peasants and gipsies and, if forced to pass a night in a town, consoling himself by wrangling with an ostler; for thirty-seven years the other sat, as assiduously as he was then expected to do, at a desk in the office of the East India Company. One was earnest, blunt, and direct, or at least liked to think of himself as such; the other, pretending to take nothing seriously, preferred the oblique approach. No two men were ever less alike than Borrow and Peacock. Yet their very differences are Welsh-like, and their points in common are not limited to their love of Wales. At all social and intellectual levels they have their passionate addicts and their bowing acquaintances, civil but constrained in manner. They are secure in their niches; but there will always be people, an unhappy few, who are in their heart of hearts a little puzzled as to how they got there.

Something of the two authors' qualities—simplicity and sophistication, tenacity and independence, eagerness for knowledge and argumentativeness—marks the Welsh nation, and something of the readers' contrasting responses—the enthusiasm and the lack of comprehension, the love and the lip-service—divides their English neighbours. The English are handicapped by certain notions which, however hot the pace of world citizenship, they are loath to discard, and high among these comes suspicion of the linguist. The Welsh are bilingual; worse, they share the island of Shakespeare and Herrick, Keats and Wordsworth, Cowper and Crabbe, whose works they are free to enjoy, while keeping for themselves a treasury of lyric and nature poems locked away for ever in their native tongue.

The defenders of native cultures are everywhere, and more than ever, up in arms; yet their opponents are numerous, undeclared and, what is worse, usually un-intentional. The border counties, once the guardians of Welsh life, are now the open doors to Anglo-Saxon views and amenities. Even in the heart of the country, people, who used to make their own music, may now have to travel forty miles to hear harp-playing of a standard that would have satisfied Owain Glyndwr. Welsh wild-fowl, hunted from lake to lake, find their way more easily to the London market than to the bird sanctuaries. Welsh farms are apt to pass into the hands of 'enterprising' men from other parts of the island. The natives will need all their persistence, all their imagination and acumen if they are to maintain their character and their way of life and, at the same time, their progress and their place.

Seventy-six water-colours were painted in Wales—fewer than was intended yet, in view of the difficulties of travel and lodging during the war, a respectable total.

TOLL HOUSE, TREWALCHMAI, ANGLESEY

Barbara Jones

A. 5, or the London–Holyhead road, has always been the main carrier of the Irish traffic, and thus one of the better, or one of the less appalling, roads. It doubtless existed, in some sort of shape, even before it was known as Watling Street. It was turnpiked in 1765. In 1822 Thomas Telford, who had been working on the Shrewsbury–Holyhead portion of the thoroughfare since 1815, reached Anglesey, where he made considerable alterations of the road in preparation for his suspension bridge, which has spanned the Menai Straits since 1826.

'With the exception of "Nant" for Llangefni, all of the five original toll-houses on Telford's road still survive—Gwalchmai (or Trewalchmai), Llanfair-Pwllgwyngyll, Llanfair-yn-Neubwll, and "Stanley" (Holy Island). A subsidiary gate at "Star" (Gaerwen) was added later. . . . These six toll-gates on the Telford road were, for five years, the last surviving gates in the Kingdom, and only ceased to function on November 1st., 1895.' (*The Royal Commission on Ancient and Historical Monuments: Anglesey.*)

The winged octagonal lodge seen here stands at a point where a road to Amlwch strikes northward from the main road; it is, perhaps, the prettiest of the group, and a few slight alterations, made since the drawing was done, have improved its appearance.

One of the other lodges still displays an old tariff board. Of its long and complicated list of charges, the following are typical examples:

> For any Horse, mule or Ass laden or unladen and not drawing, the sum of . . . 1d.
> For any horse, mule or other beast drawing any waggon or cart, the wheels
> being less than three inches in breadth, or having wheels with Tires fastened
> with Nails projecting, to pay double toll.

A hundred years ago those gates, those fees, were anything but a joke. They ignited the smouldering grievances of a half-starved population. The toll-houses, always increasing in number and often appearing on roads hitherto free and open, were a tangible and vulnerable token of the oppressive Powers. In 1839 a toll-gate in Pembrokeshire was assailed. The revolt grew. In 1843 hundreds of gates and lodges were demolished, especially in south and west Wales. The rioters worked at night, in large gangs with blackened faces, and because they wore women's clothes they became known as the 'Rebecca Rioters'.

CONWAY CASTLE AND A CORACLE

Kenneth Rowntree, A.R.W.S.

Castles at Beaumaris, Bere, Caernarvon, Conway, Criccieth, and Harlech were built by Edward I, in 1280 and the following years, to maintain his hold on North Wales. He was, according to report, in his fortress at Conway, amid the great defences designed by Henry of Ellerton, when he was presented with the head of Llewelyn ab Gruffydd. In 1399, granted too late a favourable wind and back at last from Ireland, Richard II sought to put himself on the defensive in the castle, to give his supporters a rallying point; but supplies were lacking and, accepting a safe conduct, he left to meet Bolingbroke at Flint Castle (Shakespeare telescopes the story). He was ambushed and arrived before Henry a prisoner; but the accident, if it was one, can have made little difference. In 1646 the castle was garrisoned for Charles I, but fell to the Parliamentary forces three months later. Charles II granted it to the Earl of Conway, who took the surprising and locally unpopular step of dismantling it.

'The most picturesque ruin in Wales' is not the only subject of the picture. Mr. Rowntree, painting at the mussel-cleansing station of the Ministry of Agriculture and Fisheries, found very happily, in his foreground, a coracle built on the river Dovey and in good condition. A coracle is 'a species of ancient British fishing-boat which is still extensively used on the Severn and other rivers of Wales . . . oval in shape and formed of canvas stretched on a framework of split and interwoven rods, and well-coated with tar and pitch to render it water-tight. . . . So light and portable are these boats that they can easily be carried on the fisherman's shoulders when proceeding to and from his work. Coracle-fishing is performed by two men, each seated in his coracle and with one hand holding the net while with the other he plies his paddle. When a fish is caught, each hauls up his end of the net until the two coracles are brought to touch and the fish is then secured. The coracle forms a unique link between the modern life of Wales and its remote past; for this primitive type of boat was in existence among the Britons at the time of the invasion of Julius Caesar, who has left a description of it, and even employed it in his Spanish campaign.' (*Enc. Brit.*)

MUNICIPAL COUNCIL CHAMBER, BANGOR

Kenneth Rowntree, A.R.W.S.

The old episcopal Palace at Bangor was built by Skefington, a highly active bishop, in 1508. It is true that it is now in no particular style. One wall, on the side of the prevailing wind, is of hung slate; and many other additions, renovations, and changes have been made, especially in 1810, by Skefington's successors. Yet it retains, or has acquired, an easygoing, comfortable air, it is the kind of house anyone would 'take' to. Perhaps it was precisely this lack of pomposity that caused Pennant to note, in 1770, that 'the prelate is indifferently lodged'.

About fifty years ago it ceased to be the Archbishop's residence and was bought by the Municipal Council; and its principal apartment, a large upstairs room, is now the Council Chamber. Browne Willis, writing in 1721 (and still worth consulting about Bangor) mentions 'a handsome dining-room on the first floor'. This may be that room. The late eighteenth-century ceiling has a *motif* of strings and woodwind, which may or may not be evidence of a musical interlude between the plates and the rates.

Except for a new, tiled fire-place, the chamber appears to have undergone little modification for a hundred and fifty years. Twenty-eight chairs, stamped with the arms of the Borough of Bangor, are not out of keeping with the traditions. Some people may wonder if the portraits of thirty-six aldermen are seen to advantage beneath the violins and oboes, the swirling chains and garlands of the extravagant ceiling; certainly the accommodation for press and public at the other end of the room is rather far from Browne Willis—nineteen plush fauteuils with tip-up seats. But the window behind the mayoral chair looks out on to a bowling-green that would surely have delighted Skefington.

ADDOLDY-y-BEDYDDWYR, GLYNDYFRDWY

Mildred E. Eldridge, A.R.W.S.

'The Welshman, though an aesthete, is a singing or a literary or an antiquarian aesthete, and will "Roll the Psalm to wintry skies" and sing like the here absent nightingale in a pert hard chapel with livid terra-cotta ornaments and brash red ridge tiles, and not think for a moment that he has done amiss. But the younger people are beginning to notice.' Since an eminent Welshman has thus commented in print, the visitor need no longer wait to get home before voicing his awe at the ugliness of the chapels of Wales.

How is it that the younger people are only 'beginning to notice'? It is worth while trying to answer this question. Nonconformist chapels were built in reaction against the influence of the established church; they were meant to resemble churches as little as was reverently possible; and their builders, deliberately departing from one tradition, were often without the knowledge, taste, and money to devise a dignified substitute. The nature of Nonconformity gave rise to a type of architecture which commended itself to people so occupied with worldly sin and the vanity of material things that they mistrusted the emotional appeal of Gothic and the fine manners of baroque. Their chapels are not meant to hold the mysterious shadows of the shrines of older faiths. They were built and are managed by the members, providing good education in self-government. Often they are used for meetings every night in the week. They are, and have long been, community centres.

The Addoldy (house of worship) -y-Bedyddwyr (of the Baptists) at Glyndyfrdwy is a highly characteristic structure, fronted with chocolate plaster on grey roughcast, and with squares of coloured glass, pink and honey, edging the windows. Addiction to galleries and steeply raked floors tends to give the chapels, seen from outside, their peculiar height. The Addoldy, though modified in 1841 and again in 1906, dates from 1824. It does not compete with the newest and most ambitious houses of worship, with their plush-covered, cinema-type fauteuils, concealed lights, and wall decorations of shaded distemper; yet it is, like most of its kind, notably clean, polished, and cared for.

BAPTISM IN THE RIVER CEIRIOG

Mildred E. Eldridge, A.R.W.S.

Pontfadog on the Ceiriog, a tributary of the Dee, has seen many an open-air baptism such as is here depicted. Adults of the Baptist denomination were plunged into the water, total immersion being a condition of membership. The scene is to some extent a reconstruction, a feat of memory, yet these outdoor ceremonies lasted down to 1939 at least. In some Baptist chapels tanks are now installed in the floor, and filled for the occasion with water of a temperature less rigorous than the mountain stream's. Despite this, the sect is said to be diminishing.

Borrow, of course, did not ignore so curious a custom; neither did he avoid one of his acrimonious conversations with strangers.

When I inquired how he came to feel so comfortable, he said that his feeling so was owing to his baptism into the faith of Christ Jesus. On my telling him that I too had been baptized, he asked me if I had been dipped; and on learning that I had not, but only been sprinkled, according to the practice of my church, he gave me to understand that my baptism was not worth three halfpence. Feeling rather nettled at hearing the baptism of my church so undervalued, I stood up for it, and we were soon in a dispute, in which I got rather the worst, for though he spuffled and sputtered in a most extraordinary manner, and spoke in a dialect which was neither Welsh, English, nor Cheshire, but a mixture of all three, he said two or three things rather difficult to be got over. Finding that he had nearly silenced me, he observed that he did not deny that I had a good deal of book learning, but that in matters of baptism I was as ignorant as the rest of the people of the church were, and had always been. He then said that many church people had entered into argument with him on the subject of baptism, but that he had got the better of them all; that Mr. P., the minister of the parish of L., in which we then were, had frequently entered into argument with him, but quite unsuccessfully, and had at last given up the matter as a bad job.

The seventeenth-century poet Huw Morus, 'the nightingale of the Ceiriog', and the nineteenth-century Ceiriog (John Ceiriog Hughes), the greatest of Welsh lyric poets, were both sons of this, the loveliest valley in Denbighshire.

GARN DOLBENMAEN

R. L. Young

Here is the only drawing to show a view common enough in Caernarvonshire and
Merioneth—a view without cattle, man, or any sign of the work of man's hands.
Not even one of those weatherbeaten, white or whitish houses which look as if they
were part of the natural convulsion and had been thrown up with the landscape.
Nothing but 'rocks and stones and trees', and the chattering water of the Dwyfor.
In the centre, at the back, rises Craig Garn. Moel Hebog (2,566 ft.) blocks the top
right corner, the north-east corner, of the view; blocks out all sight of Snowdon,
six arduous miles behind it and a thousand feet higher.

Garn Dolbenmaen ('stone rising to a head above a meadow') lies north of Criccieth. Since the day some ten centuries ago when a battle over stolen pigs was
fought there, Garn Dolbenmaen does not appear to have reached the news. May
its luck hold!

DDU ALLT

Mona Moore

A small, early, and famous railway line connects the huge quarries at Blaenau Festiniog with the harbour of Portmadoc. It was built to carry slate, and it has a gauge of 1 foot 11½ inches. High up along the north-west side of the Vale of Festiniog it runs, twisting and turning so often that the track attains a length of 13½ miles over a distance that measures 8 for a crow. As long ago as 1865 the beauty of the route, the views it offered of the unsurpassable scenery, led to little passenger cars being added to the service, and it became known as the Toy Railway. It owes its nickname to its size, of course; yet in other respects its permanent way recalls bold feats of engineering on the nursery carpet. At one point, near Tan-y-Bwlch, trains travelling in the opposite direction travel in the same direction, puffing side by side along the arms of a hairpin.

Travel, travelled; for the Toy Railway is a war casualty; not bombed or even blasted, merely non-essential, a useless mouth. The slate, independent of railways and harbours, is now moved by lorry; and for six summers the holiday-makers dwindled and dwindled away. The railway could be reopened, there are rumours that it will be. At the moment of writing it has not been.

The best of all its magnificent views comes near Ddu Allt, 'The Black Hill', at the quarry end. Epicures in scenery have described the country as the finest in the kingdom, as majestic as any in Europe. The low, stone, whitewashed house might, on the contrary, be matched anywhere in Wales. In a land where almost all the inhabitants—poor, primitive, isolated—wrung a meagre existence from the soil and found everywhere similar materials lying handy, it stands as an example of unpremeditated, unavoidable standardization. Some of these houses are *hafodtai*, summer dairy houses where a family, having followed its sheep and cattle to new grazing on the higher slopes of the mountains, would pass the warmer months. But this is too grand an establishment to be so categorized. Eighteen boys and two schoolmistresses, evacuated from Liverpool, were housed there when this picture was being painted in November 1941.

CHAPEL, TREMADOC

Kenneth Rowntree, A.R.W.S.

Tremadoc and Portmadoc are less than 150 years old. Their story is a model of conciseness, simplicity, and romance which, as every historian and topographer agrees, other towns would be well advised to copy.

William Alexander Madocks (1774–1828) was the son of a successful Chancery barrister, a Welshman living in Holborn. In 1791, or more probably (in view of his age) in 1798, he bought Tan-yr-Allt (Under the Hill), an estate of hanging woods on the edge of Penmorfa Marsh, in southern Caernarvonshire. He immediately set about reviving an old plan, abandoned by Sir John Wynn of Gwydir in 1625, to reclaim the waste tracts of the marshland; and between 1800 and 1807 he recovered, by means of embankments against the sea, 2,000 acres of land on the west side of the river Glaslyn. Thereupon, by a grant from the Crown and an Act of Parliament, he contrived to have all the sands known as Traeth Mawr vested in him and his heirs. Across the sands he built another embankment, reclaiming another 3,000 acres—a mile-long embankment, 100 ft. wide at the base. On the top, 30 ft. wide, he constructed a road (with toll-gate) which became, and remains, the chief line of communication between Caernarvonshire and western Merioneth, and 'obviates the danger to human life of crossing the sands'.

This great work, including the recovery in all of some 7,000 drowned acres, cost £100,000. Meanwhile Madocks had begun to build, on Penmorfa, a new town called Tremadoc (Madockston or Madocksville), again at his own expense. The plaster-fronted, stone-backed chapel shown here was erected between 1805 and 1808, being originally designed as a theatre. Playbills in the possession of the National Library at Aberystwyth show that performances of Mr. Sheridan's celebrated comedy, *The Rivals,* were given during a dramatic festival held in the first week in August 1808. In the generous fashion of that time the play, then thirty-three years old, was merely one item in a triple bill. Though members of his family interpreted Sheridan, Mr. Madocks reserved himself for *Sylvester Daggerwood, The Prize,* and *Children in the Wood.*

In the house immediately opposite the chapel Lawrence of Arabia was born.

WHARVES, PORTMADOC

Frances Macdonald

In 1809, interrupting for a moment his labours of agrarian development, Mr. Madocks, Member of Parliament for Boston in Lincolnshire, moved an impeachment of Castlereagh and Spencer Perceval, the grounds being bribery at election. It was a very insubstantial and ill-judged attack; and, though the national nerves were raw with the news of Corunna and the subsequent scandalous revelations in the case of Mary Anne Clarke, the House refused, by 310 votes to 85, even to hear the charges. Before the year was out Perceval was Prime Minister.

The building of Tremadoc went on and in 1821, with the passing of another Act of Parliament, Madocks began to provide his town, and the slate quarries of Blaenau Festiniog, with a harbour called Portmadoc. It was made fit to deal with vessels up to 300 tons—sufficient for the slate and copper ore which formed their cargo. Miss Macdonald's drawing shows some of the old wharves; the entrance to the harbour is outside the picture, away to the left where, emerging from the water, a small and rather unlikely looking island guards the approach. It is known as Ballast Island, and its unnatural aspect is due to the absence of natural origins. At the spot where it stands the incoming ships were wont to discharge their ballast, and in time the island has arisen.

Later, the Toy Railway, devised by James Spooner and costing £6,000 for each mile of its short run, linked the water-side and the quarries and set the seal on Madocks's extraordinary efforts. It was too late to save him. He had attempted too much and, 'becoming involved in pecuniary difficulties', he retired to the Continent and died in Paris, September 1828, fifty-four years old.

TAN-YR-ALLT

Kenneth Rowntree, A.R.W.S.

Percy Bysshe Shelley was a friend of Madocks, and in 1812 he rented for some months Madocks's pretty house overlooking the Beddgelert road. The poet was in trouble again. He had had two of his compositions—a revolutionary *Declaration of Rights* (Dublin, 1812) and a poem *The Devil's Walk*—sealed up in bottles and consigned to the ocean, and by so doing had 'excited the attention of the government'. It may seem to us a striking tribute to Shelley's influence, or to the literary tastes of the day, or to the Cabinet's nervousness, that a poem bobbing about in a bottle could, in so fateful a year, constitute a threat to the national effort; nevertheless, Shelley fled to North Wales.

Though the mural decorations are now whitewashed over, some of the yellow satin of the old furnishing still remains. Shelley was charmed with Tan-yr-allt, for a time; he worked on *Queen Mab,* he threw himself into Madocks's scheme. 'The embankment which, at a great sacrifice of natural picturesqueness, has redeemed from the sea the estuary of the Glaslyn . . . was battered by storms', and the financial situation was no less shaky. Shelley, offering to raise money, hurried to London, and it was during this mission that he at last met Godwin. (He had previously given the philosopher a general invitation to visit him at Lynmouth, but when the author of the *Essay on Sepulchres* was unwise enough to take the coach and journey all the way to Devonshire unannounced and with a single ticket only, the Shelleys had, as usual, left.) The search for backing seems to have failed, and Shelley returned to Tan-yr-allt. His enthusiasm for the district continued, but he began to grow weary of its remoteness, of the difficulty of getting all the books he wanted, and very weary of that embankment. 'Had you known', he wrote to a reproachful correspondent, 'the variety of the discomfitures I have undergone, you would attribute my silence to anything but neglect. I allude to the embankment affairs, in which I thoughtlessly engaged.'

His tenancy of Tan-yr-allt was abruptly ended the following February by a rather mysterious attack upon his life. Richard Garnett (*D.N.B.*) follows Hogg in dismissing the incident as an hallucination, yet Harriet Shelley swore there was a bullet-hole through Bysshe's nightgown. In any case, even an imaginary assassin was no fit mate for *Queen Mab*. The Shelleys bade Caernarvonshire a hasty adieu and crossed to Ireland.

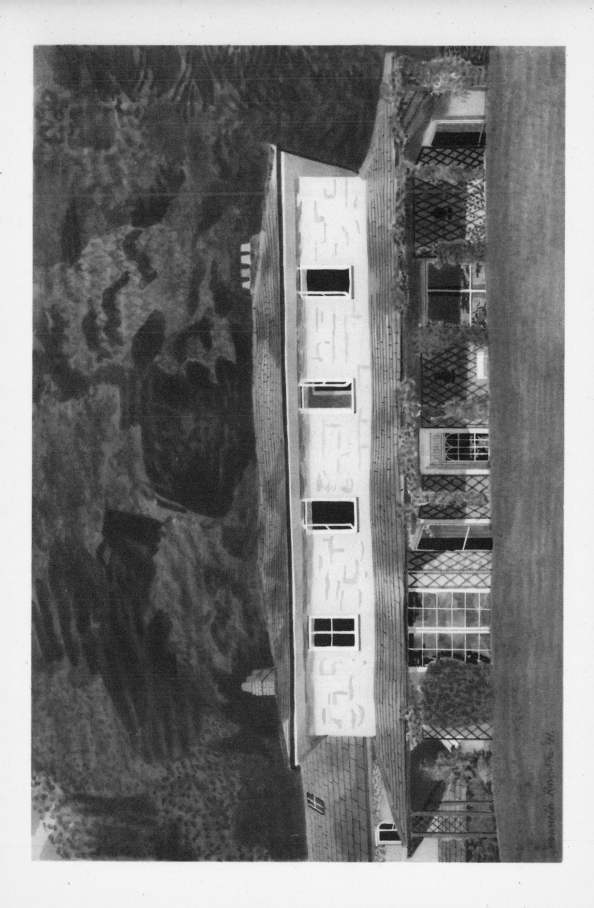

PEAT CUTTING, CEFN COCH, MONTGOMERYSHIRE

Mildred E. Eldridge, A.R.W.S.

Peat is cut and used for fuel in all the hill districts of Wales (and they are very numerous) from north to south. Most of the isolated upland farms are sited near a peat bog. In an old manuscript in the Cardiff Free Library (MS. 50) the artist found a reference to the use of peat in fulling-mills and kilns in the time of Queen Elizabeth.

There is a ritual of cutting. In early summer, in May, the peat is cut by the men, lifted by the women and children, and placed in heaps with spaces left for the winds to blow through. Later it is carried home to the peat house or made into stacks. This is done between the hay and the corn harvests, or after the corn harvest, as the weather determines.

The implement is a special, two-edged, peat-cutting iron. The peat is cut in the form of bricks, the iron shaping two sides simultaneously. The peat is lifted in rows, resulting in steps (as in the Penrhyn slate-quarry), and if the peat is plentiful the cuttings become very deep. People returning late from market have, before now, fallen into them.

PONT DOL-Y-MOCH

Frances Macdonald

Pont is, of course, the old bridge in the centre, spanning the Dwyryd stream; Dol-y-moch may be translated as 'hogs'-meadow'. The scene is in the Festiniog valley, looking north from the Maentwrog–Festiniog road.

Along the hollows at the foot of Moelwyn, at the back of the steep cliff behind the house, the miniature railway runs to the slate quarries at Blaenau Festiniog and the rocky fastness where, throughout the war, the paintings of the National Gallery of London were stored. As one proceeds north-east from Dol-y-moch, as one passes through great walls of slate holed with caves deep and black, the already magnificent scenery grows in wildness and splendour. The slate heaps blend with the rocks to such an extent that Blaenau Festiniog—built, paved, roofed, fenced, and littered with slate—fades, at a distance, in protective colouring. Some people weary of the slate; others, like Miss Touchandgo of *Crotchet Castle*, have found it restful and health-giving. Secreting her wounded heart in Merioneth, she 'was flourishing on slate while her rich and false young lord was pining on chalk'.

ST. BEUNO'S, LLAN-Y-CIL

Frances Macdonald

The ancient, but restored, parish church of Bala stands nearly a mile from the town. The churchyard runs down to the north-west shore of the lake, across which can be seen Llyn Tegid and one of the Aran peaks. Borrow, having breakfasted at the *White Lion* ('pot of hare; ditto of trout; pot of prepared shrimps; dish of plain shrimps; tin of sardines; beautiful beef-steak; eggs, muffin; large loaf, and butter, not forgetting capital tea'), accompanied the landlord—'a tall gentlemanly man of the name of Jones—oh that eternal name'—to service here one wet Sunday morning in 1854. At least, this is the church he appears to describe, though confusing Llan-y-cil with Llan uwch Llyn, four miles farther on. He quotes a legend: 'The Dee springs from two fountains, high up in Merionethshire, called Dwy Fawr and Dwy Fach . . . whose waters pass through those of Lake Bala without mingling with them. These fountains had their names from two individuals . . . who escaped from the Deluge, when all the rest of the human race were drowned, and the passing of the waters of the two fountains through the lake, without being confounded with its flood, is emblematic of the salvation of the two individuals from the deluge, of which the lake is a type.'

A tablet outside the church bears the date 1671, but the earliest of the memorial plaques within is 1726. In the yew-planted cemetery is the grave of Thomas Charles (1755–1814)—'the John Wesley of Welsh Methodism'. The British and Foreign Bible Society was founded at his suggestion; he was successful in getting a cheap Bible printed in Welsh; he became, almost in spite of himself, the organizer of Welsh Calvinistic Methodism. He had no wish to desert the established Church, of which he was an ordained member; but, again and again repudiating dissent, he was persecuted and driven from it. In 1811, by ordaining lay preachers, he reluctantly recognized and determined his separation. 'A vast concourse of people' attended the funeral, in Llan-y-cil churchyard, of a man venerated as a saint.

SLATE FENCES, ABERGYNOLWYN

Mildred E. Eldridge, A.R.W.S.

Where the slate lies ready to hand, in the slate-producing districts, it is commonly used for fencing; and, as the shapes suggest, it serves also for tombstones in many a graveyard of the older churches and chapels, and as evidence of the sure sense of beauty possessed by the craftsmen of former ages. The grey Welsh stone of the buildings and the darker grey of the slate slabs encircling them make a sober harmony, no longer to be found where modern and more ostentatious memorials are erected of black polished marble, or white, or red.

Slate, again, is used for sheepfolds and garden fences around all the principal quarrying areas—Blaenau Festiniog and Abergynolwyn in Merioneth, Corris in Montgomeryshire, or Llanberis and Bethesda in Caernarvonshire. In more portable form the slate turns up in the carved fans, thin as foliage, which decorate the black oak dressers of cottages in all parts of Wales. Then there are, or were, the slates of schoolchildren—the export of these was once four million a year.

References to slate quarrying occur in some of the accompanying notes and, on that account, it may be explained that slate is obtained in two ways, according to geological formation and age—either quarried in open face, tier upon tier on the mountain side, as at Llanberis, or mined underground, as at Blaenau Festiniog. The excellence of Caernarvon slate has been recognized since the fifteenth century. It used to be carried by mule pack, cart or wagon, sometimes by sledge carts (cair llusg) down the steep mountain slopes. Later, as we have seen, one quarry was connected by railway with the harbour of Portmadoc, and a tax on the exportation of slate by boat was lifted in 1831. Nowadays, slate travels by lorry.

THE OLD PARSONAGE, NEW RADNOR

Vincent Lines, R.W.S.

Since there is a rectory as well as an ex-rectory, it is hard to say how this sixteenth-century house acquired its name. It seems to have no right to it; according to Mr. W. H. Howse, author of several volumes of local history, it was an inn in the nineteenth century, *The Oak*. The round stone (fitted like a knee-pad to the corner of the garden-wall) deserves notice. Amid so much that is uncertain, it is reputed to be one of the stones which marked the course and distance of the trackway over which the present road is built.

The title of the drawing, though accurate enough, calls for further comment yet. New Radnor, in spite of its name, is a very old place, older than Old Radnor. The Mortimers had a castle here, the walls and moat of which were thrown round the town—if it can be called a town. In many counties it would be classed as a village. Radnorshire, though more than three times the size of the not-overcrowded Rutland, has approximately the same population. It is the most sparsely inhabited area in England and Wales; and its peace is the theme of some of the happiest entries in the *Diary* of the mid-Victorian clergyman, Francis Kilvert.

LAUGHARNE CASTLE

Martin Hardie, C.B.E.

Laugharne, one of Wales's prettiest villages, slopes down to the sea ten miles south-west of Carmarthen. As described by a writer 140 years ago, it is still 'one of the most sequestered places that can be conceived'. It was then 'much inhabited by half-pay officers, and families which seek an economical retirement'. In Elizabeth's time it was one of the six principal towns in Wales, bigger than Cardiff.

If the postman is not absent on his rather extensive beat he may produce the key to the castle, built in 1215 and the second or third to occupy the site. Brians and Devereux, Herberts and Percys have successively owned it. In the seventeenth century General Langherne took it for Parliament and then held it for the King. After a long siege, said to have been directed by Cromwell in person, it was battered into submission and partly burned. B. H. Malkins, the writer already quoted, can hardly have hoped to find the walls still smoking in 1804; nevertheless, he strongly resented the gentle efforts of the gardener. 'Not only the area, but even one of the towers, is converted to the purposes of horticulture and filled with incongruous ornaments of evergreen and flowering shrubs.' Another bygone visitor (Windham's *Tour of Wales*) took less out of himself. 'The ruins of a small, picturesque castle', he notes, 'afforded us some amusement here.'

It stands right down on the shore of a bay, at the confluence of several small rivers —the Taf, the Towy, and the two Gwendraeths. Turner drew it; he called it Langharne or Talacharne. Mr. Hardie may have been favoured with good weather; Turner, as so often, was less fortunate. It was an atrocious day. Rain lashed the towers; frenzied billows sought for openings amid a mass of storm-tossed and almost vertical wreckage; villagers, willing but helpless, lined the soaking strand. Engraved by J. Horsburgh, the plate is one of the finest of all the *Picturesque Views of England and Wales*.

MANORBIER CASTLE

Donald H. Edwards

Unexpectedly harsh judgements have been passed by some commentators on Manorbier, as if its beauty were irritant. Historians, braver than the soldiers who refrained from attacking it, have sought to remedy the uneventfulness of its career; topographers have described it as 'a jumble'.

This 'jumble' is, in fact, a narrative in stone of the main castle-building centuries, or at least of the twelfth, thirteenth, and sixteenth. Much of it is Elizabethan, but it was begun in the reign of Henry I and, though most of the Norman material has gone, the arrangement still reveals, with unusual perfection, the Norman model. It was built by Gerald de Windsor, who married the King's former mistress, Nesta, a Welsh princess. Their grandson, born in the castle, was the famous historian, topographer, and churchman, Giraldus Cambrensis, a brave and beautiful youth who declared his home to be the most perfect spot in the most perfect county in the most perfect part of the most perfect country. It was his 'House of Paradise'.

Early in the fourteenth century the fortress was seized and for a short time held by Roger, Earl of March. Otherwise, it seems never to have heard a bowstring hum or a shot fired in anger; it even kept out of the Civil War. It looks down upon the little bay whose name it shares, a few miles south-west of Tenby. It looks across some forty miles of water, still just Bristol Channel or already the Atlantic.

OLD MILL, CLYNE VALLEY

Mona Moore

Gower recovers very quickly from the anxious and gregarious holiday-makers on its eastern fringe; its interior is as rural, if not as fertile, as Anglesey's. Clyne Moor, far from being at the western end of the peninsula, lies barely a mile from the noisy tram-rails which link Swansea and the pier at Mumbles Head.

Wild ponies roam at will. A few of them have strayed into another of the artist's drawings, Oystermouth Castle. The landscape generally is rather windswept. There are few fences, and numerous barren-looking tracts, and to this lack of conventional prettiness must be attributed its immunity from the villas and motor-cars of the leaders of Swansea society. No details of the old mill have been discovered or, possibly, are discoverable, but the district is rich in folk-lore and legends (see Morgan's *Wanderings in Gower*). Borrow maintained, on the strength of the arrival, in the year 1108, of Flemish refugees diverted to this part of the country by Henry I, that the inhabitants had retained a Dutch air, and differed from the Welsh proper 'in stature, language, dress, and manners'. The great *colporteur* might have gone farther and alluded to English blood. In Gower there are plenty of people with names like Groves, Tucker, and Franklin, living in places called Cheriton, Fernhill, Reynoldston, or Middleton; and these people refer to other parts of the peninsula as 'the Welsheries'.

PENCLAWDD, GOWER

Mona Moore

Guide-books, large or small, general or local, are apt to pass over Penclawdd in silence—the utter silence of omission even from the Index. Indeed, it is an unassertive place, lacking the more obvious beauties and consisting of rows of dwellings of no great age or interest. Enjoying neither the exhilaration of the ocean nor the peace of the river, it stands on the half-hearted waters of an estuary; and from its uninviting foreshore, part mud, part sand, the tide seems always to be receding. The holiday-makers, the happy bathers, the family parties, seem to agree with the guide-books and pass it by, and even the artists seldom linger. It cannot often have been drawn. It was the very thing for *Recording Britain*.

Like Leigh at the mouth of the Thames, or like the small places on the Lancashire estuaries, Penclawdd is the home of *Cardium edule*, the common cockle—a succulent bivalve which, though conspiring with him how to load and bless our tea-tables, is not to be confused with the winkle, an edible snail. Cockles are collected by rakes drawn along the sandy bottom. Unlike oysters, they are usually boiled and extracted from their shells before being marketed.

Here, as for generations past, are the cockle-women of Penclawdd in their flannel dresses and straw bonnets. The donkeys which they rode out to Llanrhidian Sands are laden now with shells, and they and their owners drag their way home. Mounds or dumps of empty shells mark the district, here and to the east; the rather melancholy banks of the Burry or Llwchwr estuary are sometimes referred to as Cockle-land.

OYSTERMOUTH CASTLE

Mona Moore

Oystermouth Castle has long been in decay. Ivy, which has passed from the creeper category and entered the arboreal, covers, masticates, and supports it. The old fortress clings to the small steep mound that must once have daunted assailants whether from land or sea; but the presumptuous roofs of the town cage it in, and its proud, wide glare of defiance now rests upon slopes inflamed by the pink tiles of Sketty. To the crowds of sightseers hurrying to the fun-fairs and refreshment booths of Mumbles Head, Oystermouth threatens nothing worse than tea.

Things were not always thus. Ostremuere was the first of the strongholds strung out from Swansea across Gower. (The others are Penrice, Oxwich, Pennard, and Weobley, and Miss Moore drew them all.) The original construction was planned by William de Braos. This bloodthirsty descendant of one of the Norman conquerors—the lord of Braos, near Falaise—had built twenty or more castles already, but Oystermouth was destined to be his principal dungeon for Welsh or English neighbours who failed to subscribe to his ideas or expenses. He was a multiple Lord Marcher, holding no fewer than fifty-nine lordships westwards from Herefordshire.

From the beginning of John's reign he was the King's strong supporter; having accompanied his royal master into Normandy in 1200, he was given as much land as he could wrest from the Welsh in excess of his barony of Radnor. He and his wife seem to have been as large and cruel as any monsters of fable, and their children took after them. The alliance with the throne did not last; no doubt there were crimes on both sides. The end, however, is very satisfactory. The bad baron died in exile in 1211; his wife and eldest son were seized by the King and starved to death in Windsor Castle; while John himself, preferring the other extreme, succumbed to a surfeit of peaches and new beer.

It is supposed that the first castle, and its successor, were of wood, and that the existing stone building is the work of another de Braos in or about the year 1280. The lordship of Gower was presented by Parliament to Cromwell. In a survey undertaken on his instructions there is mention of 'an old decayed castle, called the castle of Oystermouth'.

132

OLD BRIDGE, BRIDGEND

Graham Bell

'The bridge at Bridgend has been rebuilt since the sixteenth century and is of eighteenth-century design. Only two arches, spanning a distance of 27 yards, are now visible, but from the pair of massive cut-waters on the upstream side it appears that other arches must exist, but are hidden by the surrounding houses. The arches are segmented in shape, and the width between the parapets is about 9 feet. The traffic is now carried by a concrete bypass bridge.' (E. Jervoise: *Ancient Bridges of Wales*. Architectural Press.)

The new bridge crosses the Ogmore at a point between the old bridge and the Wesley Methodist Church whose spire is seen in the right centre. There must have been precious little traffic through Bridgend before it was built, for the old bridge is steep, slippery with cobbles, and wide enough for only one very small vehicle at a time. Another queer feature is provided by those two 'massive cut-waters' which, instead of being both upstream, are facing in opposite directions. To-day a cut-water of the flimsiest description would be superfluous; and the differing size of the arches and the expanse of shingly shore all support the idea that the Ogmore was once a larger river in a larger bed. From some of the cottage gardens descend flights of stone steps looking as if they originally were aids to embarkation, but of little use now except, perhaps, on washing-day.

As narrow as the bridge or narrower is the approach to it, a little passage from Dunraven Place on the side of the town known as Oldcastle. The other shore, on the left, is Angel Street, in Newcastle.

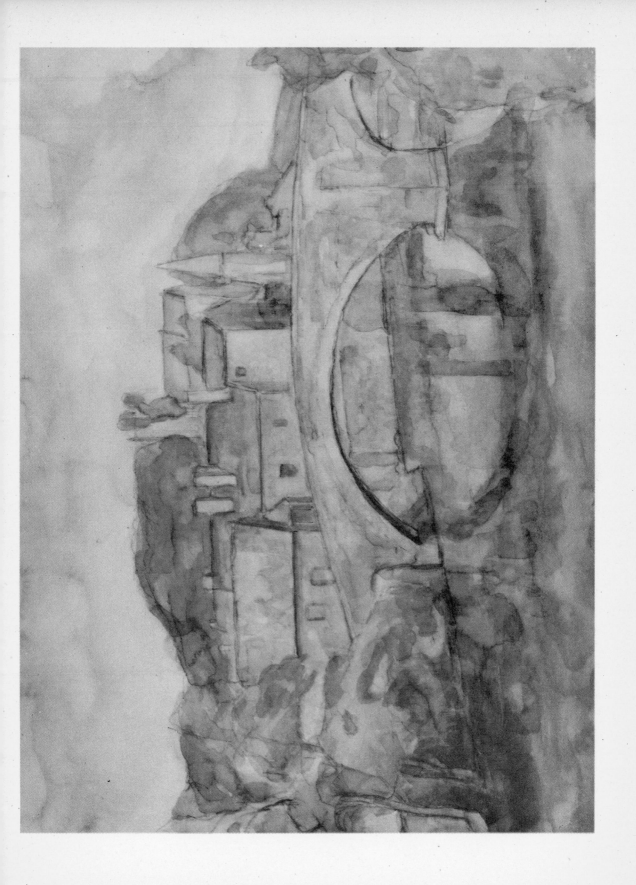

WORCESTERSHIRE

Artists

OSMOND H. BISSELL   WILLIAM GRIMMOND

RAYMOND T. COWERN, A.R.W.S.   THOMAS HENNELL, R.W.S.

E. B. MUSMAN

THE publication of the earlier volumes has brought, from some readers, evidence of curiosity and confusion about the working of the scheme. There were normal methods of procedure, yet they were, it is true, often varied; like Molière, the Committee was always ready to recognize and grasp a blessing. A brief summary is perhaps due, a scraping together of the already scattered hints.

No artists, except for the first ten or twelve needed to set the wheels in motion, were invited. The specimen works which, with applications for commissions, very quickly began and for two years or more continued to pour in, brought to light a sufficiency of suitable recorders; and this discovery of a number of talented artists, barely known or unknown, was doubly welcome. It was in spirit with the keeping of the scheme, and it removed the necessity of inviting known artists to produce, far from home, an assorted and unpredictable equipment which they might or might not have. The usual sequel to the granting of a commission is referred to in the introduction to the next county, Oxfordshire; one of the many variations may be described here. During the summer of 1942 some specimen works were received from an artist unknown to any member of the Committee. They were liked, and so was his suggestion that, from his home at Kidderminster, he should record 'some of the little humpbacked bridges and the narrow locks of the canals' of his county. He had not got very far when he was called to the Forces; nevertheless, of the few drawings that he made the two here reproduced—the locks at Kidderminster and Stourport—are examples of subjects proposed and recorded by a local artist. As an arrangement this was near to the sought ideal; subject and artist well acquainted and up to standard; a *bien* always taken and only too seldom *trouvé*.

Compared with that of many counties, the case of Worcestershire was not urgent. It is a small county, not over-industrialized. Yet it needs attention. Topographical authors and painters are apt, consciously or unconsciously, to respond to a common impulse; and anyone who visits a public library, in or out of the county, and notes how lightly Worcestershire presses on the shelves marked 'Travel and Topography' will draw his own conclusions. Twenty-six water-colours of the county were painted.

137

MILL STREET LOCK, KIDDERMINSTER

Osmond H. Bissell

When those eccentric partners Francis Egerton, 3rd and last Duke of Bridgewater, and his engineer James Brindley built the Worsley–Manchester Canal in 1761—built it, opened it, and demonstrated its efficacy—they revolutionized transport in England and made an incalculable addition to the immediate and future prosperity of the country. Roads then meant danger and expense; canals offered cheapness and safety; there were no railways. We have seen in Northamptonshire (Vol. II) the ripples of that first canal still spreading forty years later. Yet it was success as much as originality that immortalized the two oddities. Improvement of inland navigation was no new idea. Even here, at Kidderminster, a local man named Andrew Yarranton had tried as early as 1653 to render the river Salwarpe a waterway between Droitwich and Worcester; and later he nearly succeeded—coming to grief, as usual, for lack of funds—in making the river Stour navigable from Stourbridge to Kidderminster. Our Duke, in constructing a canal between Manchester and his collieries at Worsley, was realizing a dream of his father's, the first Duke.

The 3rd Duke (1736–1803) was a Lancashire-minded man, who would not entertain Pitt lest the sight of Lancashire's prosperity should suggest new taxation to the Minister. His broader-minded brother-in-law Granville, 2nd Earl Gower (1721–1803), cherished a wish to link the Staffordshire trade and Bristol Channel; and ten years after the Worsley Canal Brindley completed the Staffordshire and Worcestershire Canal at a cost of £105,000. The technical triumph was again Brindley's, but it would be a grave mistake to suppose that the Duke and the Earl were merely financial supporters of the schemes he carried out. Both noblemen played essential parts in forcing the necessary legislation through Parliament in the teeth of every conceivable opposition. Even as late as 1791, when it might be supposed that the advantages of water transport were sufficiently apparent—the Duke's canal had halved the price of coal in Manchester—the project of a Worcester–Birmingham canal was furiously fought by local business men. Living near a coal-producing area, they thought that increased facilities for dispersal would relieve the mines of surplus coal and raise the cost of fuel in Birmingham.

Such, in brief, is the historical setting of Mr. Bissell's courtyard. The Staffordshire and Worcestershire Canal, making its way past cottage doors, enters a lock, descends, and passes beneath the upper story of the house in Mill Street.

THE BASIN, STOURPORT

Osmond H. Bissell

For the basin of his Staffordshire and Worcestershire Canal Brindley chose the junction of the rivers Stour and Severn, and thus Stourport grew up. Its growth was rather slow, and even stunted. The basin was finished in 1771; but obstructionists down stream, in Gloucestershire, caused such delays that the scheme had barely reached full realization before the railways were upon it. To the passing motorist, therefore, Stourport is a small country town of limited interest; but if he leaves his car and takes a walk beside the broad Severn he will stumble—there can be few greater surprises anywhere—on 'a maritime port in the very heart of the kingdom'. The spacious basins, filled with craft of all sorts, are spread over a large area, across which one may pick one's intricate way by lock-gates and pigeon-breasted bridges.

The canal which, on entering the Severn, ended Brindley's part in the scheme was one of the first nine canals to be earmarked for nationalization. Its contrivor, the man who planned its course and led it through its endless, necessary locks—there are twenty-one at Wolverhampton alone—has caught the eye of many authors and been brought to the notice of, perhaps, most people; nevertheless, at the sight of him no writer can or ever will be able to resist digging his sharp elbow into the reader's ribs. He was the son of a small, slipshod farmer in Derbyshire, and received no education worth mentioning; yet in a far from long life (1716–72) he built the first 365 miles of our canals. He could just read; he could also write, though his spelling was phonetic and his ear inexact; but he did not favour paper-work of any kind. Calculations and specifications, all the details of his complex engineering feats were worked out and carried in his head. If a problem was exceptionally knotty, he took to his bed until it was solved. The Duke paid him a guinea a day (according to some authorities, a guinea a week), a salary which, it seems, would have satisfied him if only its payment had been reasonably sure.

The hump-backed bridge—Upper Severn Bridge No. 4, or Wall Heath Bridge—belongs to a type common not only in Worcestershire and Staffordshire but also, with little or no variation, in Berkshire, Hampshire, and wherever our old canals wander. Clearly anyone could build a pleasant water bridge whereas (though many of our most-admired river bridges are as level as a permanent way) hardly anyone has managed to build a railway bridge that is not unpleasant. The railways, if a little unlucky in their period, were one of the chief contributors, directly and indirectly, to its architectural decline.

GUILDHALL, WORCESTER

Raymond T. Cowern, A.R.W.S.

Unlike such men as Bell of Lynn and Carr of York, Thomas White (died 1738), the designer of the Guildhall, was an architect who turned to the provinces rather than a provincial architect. Wren took him from a stone-cutter's yard in Piccadilly, set him to measure the component parts of St. Peter's at Rome, and later used him as his assistant on the model for St. Paul's.

Subsequently White left London for Worcester, where he seems to have come into a little property. The Guildhall, his chief work, was completed in 1723, the year of his old master's death. It is a brick building in the manner of Wren but with more decoration than Wren was apt to favour. Reliefs, mottoes, coats of arms, statues and busts, mythological and emblematic figures fill the spaces between the yellow-gold facings, cram the niches, or stand against the sky. Some of the yellower and more important portraits were carved by the architect himself—the rather stunted sovereigns in their recesses. On the left of the main doorway stands Charles I with a model of the Cathedral in one hand, a sceptre in the other, and an ineffable smile on his lips. The corresponding figure to the right is Charles II, shaking a reproachful and tutorial sceptre at a naughty world. Above, from a position between the two central windows, looks down a furious and savage Anne. Though he may well have seen Anne and Charles II, none of his likenesses is what we have been led to expect; with or without justification, historians have preferred not to be confused by his evidence.

From the two projecting wings the central block is well set back, and the handsome railings which guard it from the street bestow additional dignity. For his Guildhall the architect was awarded a pension of £30. White built or rebuilt several of the city's churches. Travellers who know no more of Worcester than can be seen from a railway compartment must often wonder at the sight of a Wren-like tower.

Repainting the Guildhall. Worcester. R.T.Cowern. 1940

PRIORY GATEWAY, MALVERN

Raymond T. Cowern, A.R.W.S.

All places have epitomizing views, printed on the minds of the visitors and etched on the hearts of the natives. Here is Malvern's. Belle Vue Terrace opens, the houses on one side of the street disappear, the Public Gardens fall precipitously away to the lower road, revealing the Priory Church and Gateway.

The splendid Priory dates from the Conqueror's reign, and even the most perfunctory guide-book gives some account of its beauties and adventures. The Gateway (the usually misnamed Abbey Gateway arching the permanently misnamed Abbey Road) stands separated from the west end of the church; it is the only relic of the monastic quarters. Perpendicular on its northern front (seen here) and brickwork on the other, it has suffered from restorers as well as from destroyers. The structure looks as if it had lost its southern end; if so, the tradition that Henry VII lodged there becomes more credible. A weaker though not altogether negligible case for inclusion in the story can be made out also for William (or Robert) Langland, the pre-Chaucer poet. The scene of his *Vision of Piers the Plowman* was laid in the Malvern Hills; he was born eight miles away at Ledbury (see *Herefordshire*); and he may have been educated at the Priory.

Hard by the Gateway is the hydropathic establishment. To some, at least, of the seven springs of the six villages of Malvern ailing people were resorting in the time of James I; but it was not till certain doctors in the eighteenth, and still more in the nineteenth, century had developed hydropathic treatment that Malvern, in 1842, took its place among the serious spas. Of those who, in hope or desperation, sought the new cure were Carlyle, Macaulay, Bulwer-Lytton, Tennyson, and Gladstone.

Great Malvern. R.T.Cowern 1940

THE FOLEY ARMS, MALVERN

Raymond T. Cowern, A.R.W.S.

'The name of this very handsome and modern hotel', wrote John Chambers in his *History of Malvern* (1817), 'is appropriate, the ground on which it is built, with a considerable portion of the village, being the property of the Foley family. The house was built by the present proprietor in the year 1810, and considerable additions were made to it in 1812 and 1817.' He tells us that the landlord was Mr. Downes and adds, inscrutably, that 'Here is no *table d'hôte*'. A picture of Downes's *Foley Arms* shows that the house has changed little. The open-work iron supports, now seven, were five in number; there was no first-floor veranda and no bow-fronted wing. The coaching yard, now a riding school, is at the back, and at no time was it reached by the usual tunnelled way through the building.

The next proprietor was Archer, a wine-merchant, who called it *Archers (late Downes) Royal Kent and Foley Hotel*. On a printed card he offered, among other attractions, 'Excellent stables for horses at livery'; and an outside wall still bears in relief letters 'Edward Archer licensed to let post-horses and carriages for hire. Livery and bait stables.' These expressions, though in use, are disappearing. A horse 'at livery' belongs to someone staying in the hotel; he is, like his master, bedded and boarded. 'Bait' refers to casual custom; the horse is rubbed down, fed, and watered while his owner, born into a post-Downes world, enjoys the *table d'hôte* luncheon.

In the next county we shall see how prosperous inns at Burford and Tetsworth were ruined by the railways. *The Foley Arms* was luckier. The Worcester–Malvern–Hereford line was not constructed till 1860 and road traffic remained unaffected till then.. In 1852 Macaulay wrote to his friend Ellis that the supply of conveyances was 'immense. On every road round Malvern coaches and flys pass you every ten minutes, to say nothing of the irregular vehicles.' Moreover, the railway recognized instead of ignoring Malvern, and its arrival was followed three years later by the opening of the College. Two new hotels ('really palatial') sprang up, and Archer's underwent its third and most extensive enlargement. Yet even in that sanguine age there seem to have been people who turned a doubting eye on Progress. 'The visitors so misbehaved themselves that the inhabitants petitioned the railway companies against the nuisance. Certain days were fixed for trips, during which ladies and the more timid residents remained at home' (Noake's *Guide to Worcestershire*, 1868).

Great Malvern.
RT Cowern · 1940

WOOLLAS HALL, ECKINGTON

William Grimmond

Among the historic mansions of Worcestershire Woollas Hall is apt to be neglected in the guide-books; and this is strange since (in the words of John Britton or one of his numerous collaborators in vol. xv of *The Beauties of England and Wales*, 1814) 'it presents a good picture of ancient domestic arrangements', that is to say, of the days of James I. In the reign of Henry VIII or of Elizabeth—accounts vary—the estate was acquired by the Hanford family, in whose hands it remains though the name has been lost in female descent; and the existing house dates from 1611. On the right of the porch was constructed the great hall (32 ft. × 22 ft., in height 18 ft.); the chapel was set upstairs, being lit by small windows in the attic story. 'The kitchen spit is turned by a small stream of water which runs under the brow of a hill close to the house.'

The house, Britton continues, 'is built of excellent hard stone, darker in colour, and closer in grain, than that of Portland; but of which it is curious to observe, that none is now found in the neighbourhood. This is, indeed, a just subject of regret; for time has had no other effect upon it than just to give a more venerable appearance; whilst the protuberances and edges of the stone are as sharp as when first cut.' Cobbett, after being shown round by the Mr. Hanford of his day, also described the place, or began to, but was deflected into attacks on the Scottish nation, the habit of celebrating the fifth of November, and other resounding gongs.

Standing on the north side of Bredon Hill, about a third of the way up, it affords wide views over country which people, even if they have never seen it, have learned to love in the poems of A. E. Housman. According to an old book (Dr. Nash's *Survey of Worcestershire*) the area was called Wooller's-hill, a corruption of Wolves-hill, a name earned a thousand years ago when packs of wolves used the hill as their home and the country-side as their foraging-ground. There are numerous spellings of the name.

Wootho Hall near Pershore Oct 13 40
W.H.Grimmond

UPTON-ON-SEVERN

Raymond T. Cowern, A.R.W.S.

'September 19, 1851—I put Wilhelm Meister into my pocket; walked to the Cleaveland Ferry; crossed the Severn, and rambled along the eastern bank to Upton.' That Macaulay's passion for accuracy should not have covered casual jottings in his diary—that he could write Cleaveland when he meant, presumably, Clevelode—may be allowed to pass. The interesting thing about the entry is that it is here given *in extenso*, as far as Upton is concerned. Experienced and most observant of travellers, he says nothing of the magnificent tower (twelfth century) of the ruined church; or of the bridge (washed away by the flooded Severn just after his visit it must, unlike the existing sample of streamlined engineering, have been the final expected feature needed to complete the character of the little town); or of the story of Fleetwood and his eighteen men who, just 200 years before, crossed it by the single plank left by the King's sentries; or of the romantic old inns. No doubt pretty country towns were then more plentiful than now and hardly called for comment. Yet there was the bridge, and there was the church destroyed by Cromwell's men during the Battle of Upton; and there was the historian taking a few days' holiday from Volume IV.

The reason for his unusual silence is perhaps the reason for so much that is unusual in men's behaviour—preoccupation with health. Nearly a year was to pass before he consulted a doctor and learned that he could no longer rely on his strong constitution; but attentive perusal of his diary and letters reveals already some signs of uneasiness. He was 51, at the height of his intellectual power, and in the midst of a vast undertaking. At such a moment a man's perceptions may well be held by a heart-beat.

So he did not notice the *Anchor Inn* (1601), or that other bijou of an inn, the *Bell* (1688) in New Street, or even—most surprising omission of all for a man so steeped in the literature of the eighteenth century—the *White Lion*, whose projecting porch in the High Street is shown on the left of our drawing. It was here that Tom Jones, after rescuing her from the attentions of Ensign Northerton, brought Captain Waters's distressed lady; it was at this 'house of exceeding good repute, whither Irish ladies of strict virtue, and many Northern lasses of the same predicament, were accustomed to resort in their way to Bath' that there followed (see Book IX of Fielding's story) one of the fullest, most disturbed, and irregular nights in fiction.

Upton-on-Severn   R.J.Coram—1940

HEREFORDSHIRE

Artists

RAYMOND T. COWERN, A.R.W.S.   VINCENT LINES, A.R.W.S.   LOUISA PULLER

THIS almost circular county 'doth share', according to the ever-playful Thomas Fuller, 'as deep as any in the alphabet of our English commodities through exceeding in W for wood, wheat, wool, and water'; and already, in the seventeenth century, he claimed for it, on the strength of the cider for which it still is famed, the alternative title of Pomerania.

For the topographical artist, however, it is the shire *par excellence* of black and white half-timbered buildings, and very few of the thirty-eight drawings made there omitted, or could possibly have omitted, examples of the style. When, as often happens, the decayed plaster is replaced by brick, the brick is painted white; and sometimes when an entire wall—plaster, beams, and all—has perished and a solid brick wall raised in its stead, the half-timbered effect is reproduced in paint on the brick. So strong is the tradition that even new and utterly unsuitable erections are forced into line—for instance, a small hangar, added to a garage in Wigmore, has its front painted in white squares with wide black borders. By contrast, Herefordshire is poor where most counties are richest, in eighteenth-century work. Of that period there are pleasant houses in some of the larger towns and sundry fine country mansions; but one may jog all day from village to village and see scarcely a trace of it.

Although the ordinary, small half-timbered house is apt to look as if it had happened rather than been designed, on the larger structures were lavished all the elaboration and love of decoration of Tudor times. The most famous of the county architects, John Abel, achieved a national reputation. It is worth noting that he was born in 1577, and was four years younger than Inigo Jones. Unfortunately, the market houses at Leominster and Hereford, two of his finest works, were destroyed in the middle of the nineteenth century. He was in Hereford when the Scots besieged it in 1645, and the corn-grinder which he invented brought such comfort to the garrison that he was appointed one of the King's Carpenters. He designed his own monument, in Sarnesfield churchyard; according to Price's *Historical Account of Leominster* (1795), his effigy, kneeling with his two wives, was cut by his own hand; and he wrote his own epitaph, concluding

> His house of clay could hold no longer;
> May Heavens frame him a stronger.

Since he was then over 90 and lived to be 97, it is not clear whether his lines were a challenge or a complaint.

PAYTOE HALL, LEINTWARDINE

Louisa Puller

Paytoe is to be found in a thinly populated area south-west of Leintwardine. If it had not a name, one would scarcely guess that it claimed to be a village at all.

As an example of the persistence of the half-timbered tradition the Hall may be recommended, for some portions of it are at least two hundred years younger than others. A fairly long account of it is given in the third of the Herefordshire volumes issued by the Royal Commission on Historical Monuments, and from it the following details have been extracted. The east wing is of mid-sixteenth-century date. Early in the following century the main (west) part was rebuilt, and rather later the south wing was added. The small west wing is of the early eighteenth century; sundry accretions have occurred since. The brickwork is yellow in colour and, according to Mrs. Lowe, the owner, Jacobean in period. The timber framing is exposed inside as well as out; inside, too, are the old small windows looking from hall and kitchen into the sitting-rooms.

Some of the outhouses contain features belonging to the twelfth century, and Mrs. Lowe thinks that the house must originally have been built at the same time. She is also owner of the Abbey Grange, the old farm-house of an Augustinian monastery a few hundred yards from the Hall. The suggestion has been made that the Hall was once a nunnery; signs of a secret passage have been found, and the two buildings may have been connected in fact as well as in management. However, the Hall was drawn and is here presented merely for the sake of its strongly local character and appearance.

HOUSE, WIGMORE

Louisa Puller

Very quietly, during centuries of expansion and stir, Wigmore has been slipping back. Most towns can be traced to small beginnings. The once-famed Wigmore, travelling in the opposite direction, shrinks to a modest end. It lies in magnificent surroundings, precipitous enough for adventure, fertile enough for comfort; and here, in a 'chief' castle, generations of Mortimers opposed the marauding Welsh and 'made more than one English monarch uneasy on his throne', not neglecting to ally themselves by marriage with Glendower and Plantagenet. Mortimers appear in five plays by Shakespeare.

The Mortimer who helped to deprive Edward II first of his throne and then of his life must be thought to have caused that monarch more than 'uneasiness'; and during the minority of Edward III he was the *de facto* ruler of the realm. Later, another Mortimer was Heir Apparent to the Crown. Eventually, in the person of Edward IV (1461–83) the family reached the throne, and Wigmore the summit of its fortunes. It remained a royal estate until Elizabeth parted with it. It then changed hands once or twice, but she was still alive when, in 1601, it was bought by Thomas Harley for £26,000. Just over 100 years later Robert Harley became Lord High Treasurer and was created Earl of Oxford, Earl Mortimer, and Baron Wigmore; but to the grim fortress on the edge of the town there could be no revival of glory. During the Civil War Lady Brilliana Harley had wished to hold the castle for Parliament. Finding that Colonel Massie could spare neither men nor supplies for her purpose, she did what no Welsh or English prince had ever managed to achieve, and levelled the historic stronghold of the Marcher lords. Members of the medical and dental profession and their patients will learn without surprise that the Harleys of Wigmore had another estate, at Wimpole in Cambridgeshire, and that Edward Harley, 2nd Earl of Oxford, acquired property in London by marrying Henrietta Cavendish-Holles, daughter and heiress of the Duke of Newcastle.

The old house shown here seems to have no particular history. It is later than Lady Brilliana and earlier than Sir Robert; and it was either a larger house or was connected with another house running up the slope behind it. On its steep site in the middle of the town it illustrates the ground rising quickly from Watling Street to the encircling hills. From its top window the views are doubtless as far, as empty, as in the centuries before the first Mortimer.

Louisa Puller
1941

PEMBRIDGE

Raymond T. Cowern, A.R.W.S.

Villages like Kingsland, Pembridge, Weobley (now a little despoiled), and Eardisland, all lying west of Leominster, offer as good a display of domestic half-timbered buildings as can be found even in Herefordshire.

Pembridge, though no longer possessing the market rights granted by Henry I, retains notable features, such as the detached belfry, pagoda-like in shape and composed chiefly of timber, and the beautiful, open market hall (entirely wooden) which now serves uncomplainingly as a shelter for the spavined, hard-mouthed cars of farmers. The scene shown opposite is less dominating and more vulnerable. Here, at the west end of the village, the road sets off over the few remaining miles to the Welsh border, to Radnor. The separate, black and white house in the centre, in the distance, dates from the time of James I. Most of the other dwellings are much older, those on the right being probably of the fourteenth century.

Renmbridge Hertfordshire.   R.T.Cowern. 1940.

DOVECOTE, EARDISLAND

Vincent Lines, R.W.S.

For our ancestors a pigeon house was no mere home for pretty tumblers above the lawn; on the contrary, it was a serious business. In family records, such as the Verneys', we can note the degree of self-containedness which was reached on a country estate. Brewing, baking, churning, and the grinding of cereals; breeding, feeding, and killing of beeves, pigs, and sheep; poultry rearing; various activities in plantation and saw-mill, in forge, laundry, cattle shed, dairy, garden, orchard, root and apple stores; kennels and stables—all these and their attendant staffs were part of a big concern, and on them, and not on local or London shops, life depended and money was spent. Some of these features survive on large estates to this day, but features and estates tend alike to disappear.

Pigeon houses played an important part in domestic management. In his *English Social History* Dr. G. M. Trevelyan notes that, in the fifteenth century, the Fellows of King's College, Cambridge, annually consumed or sold 2,000–3,000 pigeons from a great dovecote at Grantchester; and he quotes the opinion of an early-seventeenth-century traveller that 'no kingdom in the world hath so many dove-houses'. Pigeon houses built on the ground, like the one at Eardisland, are said to have been manorial —that is to say, the owner had to possess sufficient land whereon his birds could maintain themselves. The rule was democratically intended to stop a man setting up a large, commercial pigeonry supported by other people's crops; but in practice it seems to have been difficult to regulate the proportions of pigeons to acres on an estate, or to bring home to the birds the need for good neighbourliness. The old dovecotes which we admire to-day were apt to be cursed by the small gardeners and farmers.

At Eardisland the pigeon house (north-east of the old Manor House) is a square building of red brick and timber, with a square lantern and a weathercock. It is usually, and rightly, described as Tudor, though there are features of the late seventeenth century. It seems to have been lived in. Now it is empty and rather forlorn, only its dummy windows impervious to the stones of boys. Beside it the Arrow, banked by well-tended lawns, flows through the middle of one of Herefordshire's most beautiful villages; and on its smooth surface the pigeon house gazes, as it has gazed for four hundred years, at the reflection of its gables.

BOSBURY

Raymond T. Cowern, A.R.W.S.

Visitors to Bosbury have usually been impelled by a wish to compare or contrast its large, embattled, thirteenth-century tower with other belfries similarly detached at Ledbury, Pembridge, and elsewhere in the county. Now that Mrs. Esdaile (*English Church Monuments 1510–1840*) has discovered the local sixteenth-century sculptor, John Gildon, and identified the wonderful Harford monuments as his, Holy Trinity is likely to have yet more visitors.

As one leaves the church precincts this—if one's thoughts are not too full of Gildon—is the view. Villages in all counties are apt to share a family resemblance, but it cannot be denied that, with such a profusion of half-timber, the sameness of the Herefordshire villages is as striking as their beauty. The traveller, passing in the course of an hour through ten or a dozen of them, is sometimes tempted to wonder if he is not for ever circling back to the same place.

An iron arch, holding aloft a lamp at the road entrance, is a feature of half the churchyards in England. But even the simplest of the works of men's hands are subject to the usual laws; the path that leads to perfection does not stop there. This bracket is probably eighteenth-century work. There does not appear to be anything magical about it, and anyone who cares to look, as he goes about, will find plenty of others as good. But he will notice at least as many where an effort at improvement has not come off, and a little gracefulness has somehow departed.

Bosbury - Herefordshire. 1940

R. T. Cowern. 1940

WYE BRIDGE, HEREFORD

Vincent Lines, R.W.S.

This, the oldest bridge over the Wye, is not the first of its line. There was a wooden bridge here before the Conquest, and later a Bishop of Hereford persuaded Henry I to replace it by something better. During the next 200 years, the thirteenth and four-teenth centuries, it called for constant upkeep; there is frequent mention of grants of pontage (bridge tolls), of stone from the King's quarry, of money, of '30 oaks of competent size from the King's forest', and again of stone after a disastrous flood. The Wye, so beautiful and peaceful in summer, is apt to reveal another character in winter. The always apprehensive Defoe, writing long after the present bridge had been built, noted that the Wye 'sometimes incommodes them very much, by the violent Freshes that come down from the Mountains of *Wales*'. In March 1947 only the roadway on the curving summit of the bridge was above the swirling waters.

The date of the existing bridge is given as 1490, and four of the six arches belong to that period. Possibly the task of construction was a slow one, for Leland, near the middle of the sixteenth century, seems to have seen some features of the earlier bridge. But it was certainly the bridge of Mr. Lines's picture that weathered the sieges, the sorties, and reliefs of the Civil War. Before the Parliamentary army finally captured the city, in 1645, a stone gateway had been erected at the southern (right) end, and was defended by the Governor against the encompassing Scots; and after the fighting one of the archways towards the northern end had to be rebuilt. A century later the southern arch, as can also be seen, required strengthening.

River and bridge compose from all angles, but the view shown here is, in spite of the garage, the favourite one. The cathedral tower used to carry a wooden steeple encased in lead. In 1786, when the western end of the building collapsed, James Wyatt was called in—a charming architect, but hardly the man for the job. His repair of the cathedral has met with unmixed execration; from first to last he seems to have been regarded as a local disaster; and the innocent visitor who to-day is tempted to admire the tower will be well advised to keep his opinion to himself. Allusion has already been made to the gradual construction of the bridge. The cathedral was four and a half centuries in the making—or, as one might say, founda-tion stone laid by William the Conqueror, opened by Henry VIII.

Vincent Lines 1942

MARKET HOUSE, LEDBURY

Raymond T. Cowern, A.R.W.S.

Ledbury is very rich in half-timbered buildings, of which the Market House seen here and the Biddulph mansion, out of sight on the left at the top of the High Street, are the principal examples. The old town has known plenty of excitement in its time, and was the scene of a particularly bloody defeat of the Parliamentary forces, under Colonel Massie, in 1645. But the King's men did not have it all their own way, and Ledbury, like many other places, had the embarrassing experience of being occupied by both sides, Colonel Birch and Prince Rupert alternately and more than once selecting it as headquarters. Prince Rupert billeted himself on a wealthy family, the Skynners. A remarkable sculptured monument in the parish church shows the father and the hatted mother of the Prince's host, and their eleven children.

A number of the existing houses in Ledbury must have seen and been seen by those Cavaliers and Roundheads. The Market House, for instance, was then a new and striking addition to the High Street, having been erected in 1633. It has been ascribed to John Abel, for no better and no worse reason than that he was a famous designer of market houses in Herefordshire and this is a fine market house, two-storied, timber-framed, tile-roofed. The framing on the east and north sides is square, on the west and south herring-boned.

Ledbury - Herefordshire - R.T. Cowern - 1940 -

MARKET-DAY, LEDBURY

Raymond T. Cowern, A.R.W.S.

On Tuesdays the market house ceases to re-echo to the mysterious games of little boys and becomes a shadow of its old self. Itinerant vendors unpack their cars and spread before their customers the latest novelties of Paris and Hollywood.

The artist, looking southwards as in the previous drawing, gives here a wider view of the High Street, with *The Feathers Hotel* on the right and, farther along on the opposite side, a hint of the famous elm-trees in the Biddulphs' park. In the foreground can be seen some of the sixteen posts of Spanish chestnut, with their curved braces supporting the projecting upper story of the Market House. These posts are gracefully shaped, and there is carving above the stone bases and at the bar-rests.

A brief account of the progressive stages of English market houses will be found later in the volume, in the note on the Witney Butter Cross, in Oxfordshire. Ledbury's Market House, as can be seen, contains no central pillar; yet its outer posts are disconnected, it is open and not walled in, and it thus belongs to the second or intermediate stage of development.

Market day. Lethury   R.T.Cowern · 1940

ENTRANCE TO NEW STREET, LEDBURY

Raymond T. Cowern, A.R.W.S.

Where the High Street changes its name to The Southend, a turning to the west, called New Street, leads the road to Ross. On the corner, its doorway momentarily marked by a deserted perambulator, Mr. Watkins's bootshop projects over the pavement. Five wooden pillars on stone bases support the upper story.

Some of its stucco facing has peeled, revealing that the house, like its neighbours, is of the usual half-timbered type. House and pillars bulge and lean, but the impression of insecurity is probably fallacious. These old houses seem able to bulge and lean for centuries, crazily yet with impunity. They have outlived countless thousands of newer and stouter-looking edifices.

Ledbury.   Half timber with studio facing

R. T. Cowern · 1940 ·

OLD TALBOT HOTEL, LEDBURY

Raymond T. Cowern, A.R.W.S.

From the point where this drawing was made, farther down New Street, the boot-shop and its colonnade are visible in the distance, on the right of the road.

Nearer stands the *Old Talbot Hotel*. The date 1596 appears on the panelling, but the north front was much changed in the seventeenth century, while the back of the building is eighteenth century. Round to the left in the High Street *The Feathers* goes back to 1560 or 1570, with additions of the early seventeenth century. These were Ledbury's principal hotels in Shakespeare's day; by the time the soldiers of the King and Cromwell drank them dry they were already nice old inns; and, according to a popular motoring handbook, they are still the principal hotels in Ledbury to-day.

Ledbury   Herefordshire   R.T.Cowern 1940

OXFORDSHIRE

Artists

STANLEY ANDERSON, R.A.	W. FAIRCLOUGH
A. F. T. ATKINS	MARTIN HARDIE, C.B.E.
WALTER BAYES, R.W.S.	R. K. JAMIESON
H. E. DU PLESSIS	ELLIOTT SEABROOKE

THIRTY-EIGHT drawings were made in Oxfordshire. It is anything but a neglected county, being most recordable; and, between its powerful attractions and the drag of more urgent needs elsewhere, it led to vacillation. It was often abandoned and as often returned to. Sometimes the resumption was deliberate, sometimes it came about from the tendency of the artists in neighbouring counties (even in their beloved Buckinghamshire) to wander over its borders and outside their commissions and to bring back one or two supplementary but irresistible drawings. Not seldom these were better than the planned and suggested ones, for they had their origin in a spontaneous sympathy between artist and subject.

Some critics of the first volume of the series have complained of a failure, at times, to join artist and subject in harmonious union. The criticism was not unexpected and, it follows, not entirely unfounded; but if the collection were to be reopened and augmented, the same unevenness would reappear. Hard to avoid at any time, it was unavoidable in the conditions prevailing. The scheme was worked like this. Ten or fifteen or twenty subjects were selected in an area and artists, one or two, considered appropriate to the nature of the task were commissioned. Since nobody but the artist himself can recognize a congenial subject, it was clear in advance that a few misfits would result. What was the alternative? If twenty artists had been sent to record the twenty subjects, much time would have been lost—and the Germans were daily adding to the value of time—without any counterbalancing certainty that each artist's eye would flash into a sparkle of sympathy as he stepped out of the train. Certainty? Not even probability.

Some of the least satisfactory drawings in the collection were the fruit of some of the most painstaking pairing, and many of the best were, as already described, the results of the artists' own enterprise and initiative. There is no cause here for surprise or regret or apology, but merely, it seems, for explanation. The Oxfordshire group of drawings was, perhaps more than any other except London's, subject to haphazard and unforeseen diversions of the artists, and for this very reason the standard in this county was high.

HOUSES BY THE BRIDGE, BURFORD

Stanley Anderson, R.A.

Like a handsome old gentleman sitting in the sun with a wall behind his back, Burford makes one hope it will be willing to talk. It is very willing. It seems to have made its début in the seventh century, but in this brief summary we must start 700 years later when, under Edward II, it had a very large and varied market, a growing industry in processing wool from the adjoining Cotswolds, tanneries, famous quarries, and a remunerative toll-bridge. The zenith of its importance came between 1450 and 1550, but the second half of the sixteenth century brought disaster. An Act of Edward VI deprived the Corporation of most of its property; and when, fifty years later, the Burgesses had patiently and little by little restored the situation, they were again stripped bare by an objectionable Baron of the Exchequer who, having become lord of the manor, successfully sued them for usurpation of his rights. That ended the Borough. But fifty years later and for 150 years after that (1650–1800) horse-racing made Burford the rival of Newmarket; and in addition to all the sporting and private traffic there were, after 1750, forty public coaches daily passing and repassing between London and South Wales, via Gloucester. Then, early in the nineteenth century, by a new and shorter road along the ridge south of the town, the through traffic was diverted. Again Burford languished; and when the railways chose to avoid it by no less than five miles, its end seemed sure. A writer in the *County History and Gazetteer* of 1852 tells of 'utter ruin' and 'general decay' and cries, in a burst of eloquence, 'It has the house agent for its historian.'

But there was the motor-car still to be invented; and Burford, if it has lost some of its animation, is now among the group of country towns (however small and select) never omitted by the intelligent tourist. To-day, with no fair, no market, no race-course, and no railway, there are about 1,000 inhabitants. At the height of its prosperity, the population was 800.

Besides the splendid church and the more than splendid monuments within, Burford is full of fine buildings and wonderfully free of poor ones. The doctor's house shown here stands by the old bridge, separated by the river Windrush from a cloth-mill and by the main road from the beautiful Old Vicarage. The wall on the left of the picture belongs to a low, creeper-clad house looking up the street and built by Symeon Wysdom (one of the struggling aldermen) in 1576. Of Burford's storied houses there are many good accounts, such as Mr. Hussey's three articles in *Country Life* (August 1945), volumes by R. H. Gretton, W. J. Monk, and others, and Mr. Compton Mackenzie's *Guy and Pauline*.

BUTTER CROSS, WITNEY

Stanley Anderson, R.A.

Witney, though not quite in the class of Burford, is a town of quality. The Green, which runs from the block of houses in the left centre to the church just visible at the extreme left of the drawing, is flanked on both sides by merchants' houses of the eighteenth and early nineteenth centuries; and these and the factories and offices, here and elsewhere, of the manufacturers of the famous blankets give character generally to the scene and satisfaction individually to the eye.

The turret of the Butter Cross, beneath the Lamb and Flag of the weathercock, bears clock-faces on two sides, a sundial on the third, and on the fourth a circular board with the inscription 'Erected by Gulielmus Blake, Armiger de Coggs, 1683'. Coggs is a suburb of Witney. The building rests on thirteen stone pillars rising from a stone floor. Oak beams, lying across the top of the central pillar, support a raftered roof; at the base of this pillar are the usual steps, serving as seats or platforms. Although restored in 1811 and 1842, the Cross has doubtless retained its main features, which may be compared with those of another unpretentious Butter Cross at Oakham in Rutlandshire (see Volume II). Both these crosses belong to the second of the three well-defined stages in the development of market centres. The first type was an open affair, a cross or column on steps of any number from two to (in one instance) twelve. In the next stage the space was roofed over, as at Witney and Oakham. In the final form the centre column and steps were omitted to give more room; instead of outside pillars, a continuous wall was built; and the result was a market hall or house.

The archway in the foreground on the right of the drawing belongs to the old Town Hall. Though thin-voiced purists may move their ashen lips in finding fault with the cluster of houses islanded behind the Butter Cross, the whole scene, shown and suggested, offers an example of planning notable for its simplicity, its spaciousness, and its unforced dignity.

STANLEY ANDERSON · 19 ·

ENTRANCE TO BOTANICAL GARDEN, OXFORD

Walter Bayes, R.W.S.

Before the Jews—16,511 in number—were expelled from England in 1290, the site was a Jewish cemetery. When, in 1622, the University received £250 from Henry Danvers, Earl of Danby, for the purchase and development of the five acres 'with a view to the general improvement of learning and especially the faculty of medicine', it had been a garden for a hundred years already, laid out by Thomas Linacre, physician to Henry VII and Henry VIII. But now it was stocked with herbs and provided by the founder with an income; and presently the *herbaria* of Dillenius and of Sherard (according to Linnaeus the most valuable botanical record in the world) were added. Later, it seems that the plants were arranged on the systems of Linnaeus and Jussieu. It is our oldest Physic Garden and, if no longer heavily leaned upon by the Faculty of Medicine, it remains a charming retreat. Through minor gateways in its 14-foot walls one passes to the river or to a smaller garden with views of the Meadows. At one time there were monkeys, too; Murray's guide-book for 1860 notes that they 'are periodically fed by the undergraduates with boxes of cigar-lights'. The first gardener being a Dutchman, he followed the Dutch custom of planting two yew-trees as protecting giants; they are still there.

On 25 July 1632 the Vice-Chancellor, after two orations, laid the first stone of the rusticated archway. It cost upwards of £500. Beneath the presiding bust of Lord Danby runs an inscription in Latin; and such is the pregnancy of that tongue that, in eighteen words, suitable references are made to God, Charles I, the University of Oxford, the Nation, Lord Danby, and the date.

Five months after the opening ceremony there was born in Oxford Anthony Wood, antiquary and historian of the city. In his *Athenae Oxoniensis*, published late in the century, he was held to have libelled the Earl of Clarendon. Wood was fined and, rather obscurely, the money was spent on statues for the niches of the gateway—to the left, a Romanized but bewigged and easily recognizable Charles I, on the right a togaless, a wigless, an unrecognizably brisk Charles II. The gateway itself, sometimes ascribed to Inigo Jones, is by Nicholas Stone (1586–1647), a mason often employed by Jones, notably on the Banqueting House at Whitehall and the watergates of Somerset House. York Water Gate is his, in Buckingham Street, Strand. Hardly excelled as a sculptor of church monuments, he designed the Italianate south porch of the University church. Its barley-sugar pillars are a familiar feature of the High Street; its statue of the Virgin and Child was the basis of one of the chief articles in the impeachment of William Laud, Archbishop of Canterbury.

35 BEAUMONT STREET, OXFORD

Stanley Anderson, R.A.

Beaumont Street's name goes back at least 800 years to the Palace de Bello Monte built on the site by Henry I in 1153. Henry II found it handy for Woodstock and fair Rosamond Clifford; he and succeeding kings continued to use the palace until Edward II, as the result of a panicky vow (not the only one) made to a friar at Bannockburn, granted the establishment to the Carmelites. Even then, and for some time to come, any monarch visiting Oxford continued to expect and to obtain accommodation at the Palace. There is much more of the early and middle chapters of the story, easily discoverable by anyone who cares to look—rather more easily, indeed, than some of the concluding pages. It is known, however, that Worcester College, founded in 1714, had only one approach, through 'Friar's Entry' opposite St. Mary Magdalene's Church; and that 'the opening of Beaumont Street and introduction of Worcester to the civilized world' was the price demanded by that college for its support of the Parliamentary representative of St. John's, the landlord college at the other end of the street.

The lady who seems to have risked or to be about to risk leaving her bicycle unattended in an Oxford street and the old gentleman gazing at her with such natural incredulity have halted by the doorway of Barnett House. This building is the home of various offices for the study of social welfare; and, like the Trust to which it is leased, it bears the name of the founder of Toynbee Hall. In some twenty years' time it and its neighbours are due to be demolished and replaced by a very large extension, westward to St. John Street, of the Ashmolean Museum.

Unfortunately they are not quite old enough to impress public opinion, in its present stage of development, with their importance. Nevertheless they are, within and without, admirable examples of the town houses of their day—1825, the eleventh hour of domestic architecture in England. The name of the architect has not been discovered; at such a time, in such a city, the possibilities are numerous. Blore is one, and so is Smirke's pupil, Henry Jones Underwood, whose lodge, library, and lecture room at the Botanical Garden, though they rob Stone's arch of its full effect, are worth notice. But if these houses are compared with others of the very same year (see Grosvenor Road, London, and Albion Place, Reading, both illustrated in Vol. I) the reader may decide that the architect hardly matters, that he perhaps never existed save as compiler of a pattern book.

STANLEY ANDERSON · 1941

HOUSES, THAME

Stanley Anderson, R.A.

The road between Aylesbury and Oxford is very well treated by Thame. It is awarded great breadth and bordered almost exclusively with fine houses. True, a good many of them have now only their upper stories; the ground floors are adapted as shops. Nevertheless, Mr. Anderson could have made numerous, and did make some, drawings of other surviving and charming residences, or at least of houses which have kept their front doors. Some of the shops, too, must always have been shops.

The houses shown on the opposite page are typical. No particular history attaches to them, they are merely the homes of generations of better-class residents. They stand at the widest part of the wide street, south-east of the Town Hall and the house to which, in 1643, John Hampden found his way, half-dead with wounds, from Chalgrove Field. 'With his head hanging down, and his hands resting upon his horse's neck, he at length arrived at the house of Ezekiel Browne, in the street of Thame.' In this house, once Browne's, once *The Greyhound Inn*, once a butcher's shop and now a hosier's, 'through six days he lay dying, and round the bedside of that Captain, upon whom his bitterest enemies could fasten no other action of disrepute but that he was too zealous a Christian, were gathered many of those who loved his cause and honoured himself'.

Often, in our small towns, the Town Hall is the sole remaining building of worth. In the beautiful street of Thame it is the chief disaster. In writhing letters cut on a stone panel it makes the twin boast of occupying the site of the old market hall of 1579 and commemorating the Jubilee of Queen Victoria. Islanded and stertorous red it stands, seeming to have been sent to Coventry by its neighbours and, in its unregeneracy, to prefer it so.

STANLEY ANDERSON 1941

THE SWAN, TETSWORTH

Stanley Anderson, R.A.

On every day of the week six-and-twenty coaches, rumbling along the main road between High Wycombe and Oxford, used to pass through Tetsworth or to pause there for refreshments and a change of horses. It is some twelve miles from either place, and made a convenient half-way house for hired post-chaises and private carriages as well as stage-coaches. Traffic was brisk and supported two inns. Since *The Swan* is at the Oxford end of the little town and on the left of the road for eastbound travellers, we may indulge in the belief that it was here that, one night late in October 1821, three Irish ladies descended. Maria Edgeworth and her sisters Fanny and Harriet, after sight-seeing in Oxford and attending evening service at 'Maudlin', had resumed their journey to Wycombe Abbey.

'Good tea at Tetsworth; amused ourselves next morning reading like ladies, and watching from our gazabo window the arrival and departure of twelve stage-coaches, any one of which would have been a study for Wilkie, besides the rubbing down of a horse with a besom; at first we thought the horse would have been affronted—no, quite agreeable. The dried flakes of yellow mud, first besomed and then brushed, raised such a dust, that in the dust, man and horse were lost.'

The days of that picturesque scene were, though nobody knew it, already numbered. There was stabling for forty horses at *The Swan*; yet by 1852 'the wheels of but one solitary coach are only heard to rattle through the streets of Tetsworth'. The commentator in the *County of Oxford Gazetteer and Directory* goes on to say that *The Royal Oak*, the other inn, 'has been pulled down; *The Swan*, another good inn, is converted partly into a post office, and partly into a warehouse'. The prosperity of Tetsworth was ended; and to the inhabitants it must have been an added mortification that the railways which ruined it seemed never to have heard of it. For its twenty-six coaches it received not even one train a day. It is still without a station.

The Swan is once more an inn, that is to say, it has a bar; but the discerning and hungry voyager, his eye caught by traces of successive centuries in the fine old house, will be told to take his appetite two or three miles along the road to an establishment where, though the old hospitality prevails, surroundings are olde. It was this contrast, perhaps, that led to the following entry in a recent guide-book: 'Swan Inn is a red-bricked, winged building, untouched. Preserve it from road-house "development"!' Unfortunately, it is not being preserved. It is falling into disrepair.

STANLEY ANDERSON 1940

WHITE POND FARM, STONOR

W. Fairclough

The village of Stonor lies two or three miles to the north of Henley whence, to reach it, one goes by Bell Street and the stately avenue known as the Fair Mile and then, shying at Bix Hill, turns to the right. Hambleden, Fingest, and other places appearing in the Buckinghamshire section of Volume I are only a short way to the east.

Stonor gave its name to a family living there before the Conquest, and members of this family and bearers of this name are still living hard by. (See, for some of the intervening history, the *Stonor Letters*, published by the Camden Society.) White Pond Farm stands at the northern end of the village, in the wedge of the Watlington and Turville Heath roads. No further comment seems called for, or none that the reader cannot supply for himself with Mr. Fairclough's aid.

White Barn Farm, Simion
(2) Fairclough.
July 1943.

UPPER ASSENDEN FARM, STONOR

W. Fairclough

Upper Assenden Farm (Mr. Hunt's) is at the opposite, the southern, end of Stonor. This well-kept property, with fine, oak-timbered barns of great if (as usual) uncertain age, makes a charming group, whether seen from the back, as here, or from the road front. Of a picturesque South Midland farm it would not be easy to find a better or more genuine sample.

The ground rises all round it but, as the drawing shows, especially to the north. There can be seen, beginning, the steep hillocks and sharp declivities so characteristic of the country in which Fingest lies withdrawn.

Upper Brendon Farm. Devon.

D. R. Clough.
August 1943

ST. JOHN THE BAPTIST'S, MONGEWELL—EAST END

W. Fairclough

A private road ends at a double gateway of wood. Rather stiffly, the doors admit us to a stable yard, deserted, long deserted. As we venture questioningly forward there is not a sound, even of our footsteps. We cross to the far end; and there we have, for a moment, the choice between the silent stillness of death and the snarling, raging fury of life.

We go on. Parting the boughs from our path and the clinging tendrils from our faces, probing and peering through the dark entanglement, we see ourselves in a cartoon by Burne-Jones, one of those pale and sensitive figures who, born in a poem by Morris, Tennyson, or Dante Gabriel Rossetti, is now half-way to a dim, enormous, tapestried end. Lacking his protective armour, at every step we halt and ease, carefully and patiently, our clothing from the barbed bramble. We are in the churchyard of St. John the Baptist's, catching a glimpse every now and then of a green and throttled tombstone; and in due course we come to the half-prone door and rolling rubble of the south porch of the church itself. A wild and desolate scene greets the eye. Branches have thrust their way through windows and roof, and creepers, like fussy draperies, swing in mid-air. Their slow, determined entry is marked by powdered lime and glass on the floor, sometimes heaped, sometimes scattered, and sometimes fallen into the gaping holes of the dry rot. One moves about warily, always ready to transfer, on an instant, the weight to the other foot; and even this gentle progress in a building once described as 'massive' is now felt by the roof and calls down a dusty snow. The icy air, searching frantically for warmth, presses itself against one's body.

The Norman arches to chancel and apse were restored in 1881. Victorian tiles of hygienic appearance line the chancel steps. There seems to have been a central heating system. Monuments show that funeral services were held here as late as 1934.

A private or semi-private place of worship, it served the big house on the far side of the lawns, the flower-beds, and the ornamental water. Beside the Thames sliding down from Wallingford to Goring the mansion (listed by Cassell's *Gazetteer* as 'a seat') stands hale and hearty, if requisitioned. Why has the little church fallen into decay so utter and sudden? The neighbouring rector is a new-comer; the owner of the house is beyond reach; the books are silent or summary; and the answers to our questions, though no doubt they exist, are receding into the distance and will soon be gone.

Mongewell Church
September 1940
W. Fairclough.

ST. JOHN THE BAPTIST'S, MONGEWELL—WEST END

W. Fairclough

Signs of the trespassing vegetation may be seen in the drawing. Here, at the western end beneath the singular bell turret, decay is more rampant than at the restored eastern end; but throughout the edifice, and especially in the floor, it has spread and increased since these recordings were done in August 1940. The church then had not lost all hope, all self-respect. Now its extinguished spirit no longer flickers.

The Saunders family (*temp.* George II), to whom the chief monuments belong, must be passed by in favour of Shute Harrington, Lord Bishop of Durham, who died in London in 1826 and is buried beneath the font. From a board opposite, on the north wall, we learn that he 'anxiously promoted the welfare and comforts of the cottagers and poor of this parish during the 55 years he was Lord of the Manor', and for once the composer of the epitaph was able to advance evidence in support of his claims. By a Deed of Trust dated 1809 the good bishop provided an annual income of £70 for the maintenance of the free school and for the placing out of the poor children of the parish to trades, 'if expedient'. In addition, there was a third call on the annuity—the support of the village shop which the bishop had established—and it is this that has given rise to the interesting and serious contention that the first beginnings of the co-operative movement are here commemorated.

The handle of the besom lies across a step to a chapel or vestry containing other tombs. All the interior of the church, or all but an inch or two, is shown in the drawings, the right side of one joining the left side of the other.

W. Fair. del.gt.
Langwell Church
August 1910.

BELL STREET, HENLEY-ON-THAMES

W. Fairclough

Henley, like Newmarket, has learned to watch its visitors come, pay, and go. It has kept its head, survived its own attractions, and, in spite of being labelled Mecca and Metropolis, has remained a country town.

Good buildings, buildings which look as if they had a history, are spread all over it, the best concentrations occurring in Hart Street, Bell Street, and New Street. Here are some, but only some, of the handsome residences of varying ages, shapes, and sizes which form the northern entry to the town. The row, stretching away to the left, includes a large building now divided into five houses and once famous as *The Bell Inn*. During the Civil War the King's brilliant nephew, Prince Rupert—an Elizabethan figure overrated by schoolboys and underrated by almost everyone else—used it as his headquarters and the elm in front of it as a gallows for spies. There is a tradition, however, that he billeted himself in one of the two large houses facing us in Mr. Fairclough's drawing; and as Rupert House it continues to be known. It and its neighbour were extensively reconditioned, if not positively rebuilt, in the time of Queen Anne, but houses have occupied the site for a very long time. The adjoining building is still called The Countess's Garden, though it is nearly 700 years since a Countess of Cornwall walked in that garden.

Bell Street
Henley-on-Thames
W. Fairclough April 1942.

HENLEY BRIDGE

W. Fairclough.

William Hayward of Shrewsbury designed but, dying at the age of 41, did not live to see this five-arched bridge. It was completed in 1786. Horace Walpole, in two letters written that summer, declared 'there is not a sight in the island more worthy of being visited' and called it 'the delight of my eyes'.

It is beautiful, even if Walpole was prejudiced by his affection, from her infancy till his death, for Anne Seymour Damer who carved the masks on the keystones—a matted and reedy Father Thames facing downstream, and a smooth Isis on the Oxford side. 'Long with soft touch shall Damer's chisel charm', sang Erasmus Darwin. Unfortunately *The Economy of Vegetation* has lost readers of late years; the Hon. Mrs. Damer possibly interests us to-day less by her art than by her character. She was one of those well-connected, advanced, spirited ladies in which our country always has been and still is rich. Her mother was the daughter of the 4th Duke of Argyll, her father was Field-Marshal Conway of Park Place, hard by Henley Bridge. She thus started with 'every advantage', and seemed to fortify her position when, at the age of 18, she married John Damer, heir to Lord Milton and £30,000 a year. In 1776, having contracted debts which his father refused to honour, her husband shot himself. His wardrobe was sold for £15,000. Left with an annual jointure of £2,500 his widow devoted herself to the art in which, even before her marriage, she had attained some proficiency. Fox was her friend, and so was Josephine Beauharnais who invited her to Paris during the brief Peace of Amiens and introduced her to her husband. Mrs. Damer promised Napoleon a bust of Fox and, what is more, she delivered it twelve years later, during the Hundred Days, receiving in exchange a diamond snuff-box with the Emperor's portrait. George III and Nelson sat to her (she gave a copy of the Nelson to the King of Tarjore 'to wean the Hindoos from the worship of ugly idols') and she presented a bust of herself to the Uffizi Gallery. Meanwhile, Horace Walpole had left her Strawberry Hill for life and £2,000 for its upkeep. In 1800 she produced Mary Berry's *Fashionable Friends* at Drury Lane and herself recited the epilogue by Joanna Baillie. In her seventieth year she bought York House, Twickenham, and there, amid her busts and terra-cottas and her mother's worsted work, the lonely Queen would come for a chat.

The view, from Jack Arlett's wharf, shows the Old Angel Hotel and pleasant houses of Thames Side, and the fifteenth-century tower of St. Mary's Church. The regatta course is on the other side of the bridge.

GLOUCESTERSHIRE

Artists

STANLEY ANDERSON, R.A.	A. M. HIND, O.B.E.
GEORGE BISSILL	LOUISA PULLER
PHYLLIS GINGER	MICHAEL ROTHENSTEIN
A. S. HARTRICK, R.W.S.	W. E. SPRADBERY
THOMAS HENNELL, R.W.S.	ROBERT SWAN

LORD YPRES

AT first Gloucestershire's place on the list of urgencies was a lowly one. The county seemed to us, in our innocence, far enough to discourage visits from air raiders; and since its scenery and its buildings have always attracted artists—amateur as well as, even more than, professional—it was supposed to be in no great need of recording. Both notions proved ill-founded. The Germans soon showed that they knew all about Bristol, including how to get there; and Gloucestershire turned out to have, like every other county, appropriate subjects sufficient for generations of recorders yet to come. If numbers be taken for a test, it ended, after its slow start, by occupying the ninth position in the collection. Sixty-five paintings of the county were done.

The chief recording centres were the Cirencester–Quenington area in the east; in the south, Clifton and Bristol, though much of the great city had gone by the time the artists got there; and a curving strip down the middle of the county, from Winchcomb via Cheltenham and Stroud to Tetbury. Other places are represented in the collection, but these were the scenes of the principal activity. The Forest of Dean, west of the Severn estuary, had to be omitted.

For every drawing reproduced in these volumes three have to be left in their frames or portfolios. However carefully the task of selection is accomplished there results inevitably a diminution of scale, a change in the proportions, of the scheme. No mere list can remedy this; nevertheless, it may be worth while for once to give an idea of the subjects of some of those other drawings in the county group. A famous oak-tree, at Lassington; the old home of the Hoare family, members of which sailed on the *Mayflower*; a cart horse with 'housings', i.e. a large flap of thick leather intended to keep rain off the animal's shoulders; a small, local pottery, still surviving; a breast plough, a wooden furrow-maker strapped to the ploughman's waist and pushed by him through the earth; two early Victorian railway stations.

TITHE HOUSE, GREET MANOR FARM, WINCHCOMB

Thomas Hennell, R.W.S.

Not long after he had completed this painting the artist left for the South-East Asia
theatre of war. It is, therefore, one of his last pictures of the country he knew and
loved so well, and was never to see again. He had a beautiful habit of writing long
letters, on immense sheets of paper, describing what he meant to do, was doing, and
had done; and after mentioning in one of these (14 April 1943) that he had taken
with him 'an old beginning of what appears to be a pigeon-tower, but is called the
Tithe House, at Greet Manor, about a mile away', he returned to the subject in the
course of a letter written eight days later.

' "Winchcomb" is the spelling insisted on by locals, though I think it has an *e* in some
maps as well as in Baedeker. . . . I can't say much about the Tithe House. Nobody
seemed to know its history, and the farmer's wife denied that it had ever been a pigeon loft
(which it obviously had). It belongs to Mr. Wm. Hall, Greet Manor Farm, whose perry
is uncommonly good, though stronger than it tastes.'

Hennell was a man of boundless curiosity and precise knowledge of many and
varied matters; and it is not surprising that further attempts to trace the history of
the tithe house have merely confirmed his 'nobody knows'. The building, of brick
and stone, is clearly of considerable age. Though it has undergone slight adjustments
for farm use (its ground floor is now a hen-house) it has not suffered restoration or
renovation. The nine worn steps mount to a door giving access to the main apartment, now a storeroom but possibly once (if there is any basis for the building's
name) the scene of the acquittal of tithes. There was an abbey at Winchcomb,
destroyed after the Dissolution, and this has led some people to believe that the tithe
house may be an outlying survivor of that foundation. 'Simply an opportunity
taken,' runs the note accompanying the drawing, 'and not work done by request.'

MUSIC GALLERY, BISHOP'S CLEEVE

A. S. Hartrick, R.W.S.

Within and without, St. Michael's Church, a twelfth-century building, has many notable features, and one that is surely the supreme example of its kind—the early seventeenth-century gallery at the west end. It is of carved oak, the front of the main beam being especially elaborate; and the front columns have turned mouldings. Inside it, at the back, is another gallery, smaller and narrower, to which access is given by a short staircase from the main gallery.

The orchestra—oboe (or 'the horse's leg'), first and second violin, and bass viol, with a pitch-pipe to give the key for psalms and hymns—occupied the inner, smaller gallery until the day when Bishop's Cleeve, like other English villages, turned out the musicians, turned out its pockets, too, and bought an organ. That was in 1859. It seems to have been placed in the orchestral pen, the choir continuing to hold its position in front.

Fuller allusion to the discarding of village orchestras was made in the note on Ridlington, in Rutland. The associations so lightly broken in or about the year 1860 were often of long standing. Before the Jacobean gallery there was, in St. Michael's, a large pew high up on the west wall, where the chosen singers sat with the instrumentalists. The sixteenth-century oak pews, visible beneath the present gallery, belong to the days of that earlier arrangement. Narrow, uncomfortable, devout, and even slightly bigoted, they retain their strength unimpaired, showing no sign of wearying in well-doing.

THE PROMENADE, CHELTENHAM

Phyllis Ginger

Under the Stuart kings certain spas, notably Tunbridge Wells, rose to fashion; there was another boom in the seventeen-eighties; and the development of hydropathic treatment brought places like Malvern and Matlock into the picture about 1850. Cheltenham, with Clifton and Buxton, belongs to the middle era, when the success of Bath produced, as a kind of mouth-watering, a flow of terraces, crescents, squares, gardens, hotels, assembly rooms, and pump houses.

The qualities of the spring that brought prosperity to Cheltenham were first appreciated in 1716, but for fifty years or more the commercial development, though steady, was slow and amateurish. Handel and Dr. Johnson were among the visitors. By 1780 they numbered 400 a year. All the same, one must have felt very ill indeed before taking the cure at Cheltenham. The river, serving as a sewer brook, ran down the High Street, and 'in a scarcity it stagnated and was offensive'. One crossed the street by stepping-stones; the gutters were cleaned by bundles of straw dragged on a string. That was Cheltenham in 1786, the year the houses were first numbered. Yet two years later the royal physicians felt justified in prescribing the waters for George III. The royal party had to be very small (fifteen years later there were still only thirty lodging-houses in the place), but Fanny Burney was among them, and she was able to describe the main street as 'extremely clean and well paved'. The King spent a month there, from mid-July to mid-August. The visit is said to have benefited him. It did even more for Cheltenham.

Hardly a town in England has made better use of its opportunities. During the next decades it showed, in a manner deserving our closest attention, what a garden city can become. Its period is not all it might be—Wellington, Vittoria, Rodney, Carlton, and Trafalgar are apt to be the names of its streets and residences, but there are also Alberts, Victorias, and Imperials—and Cheltenham should be regarded as a superior Belgravia rather than as an inferior Bath. It combines the grand manner of Regency England with the rural informality of continental spas like Homburg and Aix-les-Bains. The Promenade was constructed in 1818. Here, from a point between the Queen's Hotel and Clarence House, with beautiful gardens and a traditional bandstand on the right, it runs northwards, arched over by lime, chestnut, sycamore, and plane trees.

MONTPELLIER WALK, CHELTENHAM

Phyllis Ginger

For Bath's Ralph Allen, Cheltenham had several backers such as Joseph Pitt; for Beau Nash it had first Simeon Moreau and then James King; and, instead of Wood and his son, it had a number of architects, John Forbes, G. A. Underwood, the two Jearrads, and J. B. Papworth. The cooks were not so few, the menu was not so simple, the guests were not in such good time, the repast was not quite so hot.

In the decade 1817–26 the southern end of the town blossomed into a Pump Room, a Rotunda, and Montpellier Walk—new, fashionable, and by Papworth. John Buonarotti Papworth was the second son of Sir William Chambers's ornamental plasterer, and was much the most important of the architects of Cheltenham. (Professor A. E. Richardson has bidden us look for Papworth's guiding hand even in buildings not ascribed to him, like the Queen's Hotel erected in 1837, on the site of the old Imperial Spa, to the design of R. W. Jearrad.) In the new Montpellier quarter (as is the way of spas), assemblies, routs, baths, and waters offered, side by side, their mutual correctives. A glimpse, amid the glittering crowd, of the Duke of Wellington shows that great man taking his cure with characteristic thoroughness. He visited the Montpellier baths daily at 4 o'clock; spent an hour in the warm water reading eight or nine newspapers which he brought with him and propped on a frame; then, we are told, he returned home to dine and, though still far from insensible to social pleasures, rarely went out again.

No one who has ever seen Montpellier Walk is likely to forget it, for it has features all its own. Though the shop fronts have lost their old look, Rossi's caryatides—large female figures with arms shorn off above the elbows—still divide them, still sustain Papworth's upper floors the whole length of the terrace. At the far northern end, where the pavement continues through the east-projecting building, there is a notably graceful curved termination. Almost contemporary with Montpellier, the Pittville Spa Pump Room was rising on the other side of the town. With development so rapid it is small wonder if, occasionally, an enterprising man misjudged the pace. Early in the nineteenth century Jonathan Wildey thought the time had come to establish a hire service of sedan chairs. No doubt some slower thinker profited later from his idea; but Wildey went bankrupt.

THIRLESTAINE HOUSE, CHELTENHAM

Phyllis Ginger

A classic structure of the Ionic order, adorned with panelled reliefs and statues in niches, the house stands close to the high wall screening it from the Bath Road. It is best seen from the large garden at the back, although the old stable yard competes there for the attention.

It was built, to his own design, by a Mr. J. R. Scott. He had spent £84,000 on it by 1833 when, money and life exhausted, he left it 'very unfinished'. The property was bought by the 2nd Lord Northwick, who added two wings for the display of his pictures. His collection was a famous one; but Thirlestaine House had yet to learn what a collector was like. His lordship died, the pictures were sold (1859), and Sir Thomas Phillipps moved in. The following account is based mainly on an article by Edward Kite in *Wiltshire Notes & Queries*, Dec. 1908.

Phillipps was born in Manchester in 1792, only son of a wealthy manufacturer. From his father he inherited Middle Hill, near Broadway, where he lived a curbed existence until his wife's death in 1832. Even at Rugby he collected books (his schoolboy catalogue exists), but now he emerged in full rampancy. 'I began', he said, 'by purchasing everything that lay within my reach', and as he began so he continued, only his reach changing. There was not a bookseller or auctioneer in the British Isles, and very few in Europe, who did not know him and ply him with lists. At home he kept a press, a printer, a bookbinder, and his own three daughters permanently occupied. He bought ceaselessly and enormously—whole libraries and collections and, once, the entire contents of a catalogue, 1,400 volumes of manuscripts. Vellum was his especial weakness. He bought a few hundred pictures, too. By 1843 he had spent £100,000, and he went on buying for another thirty years. The collection was kept in boxes, locked and piled, with the near side hinged at the bottom. By 1859 Middle Hill was bursting with books; even Phillipps noticed it and, while still able to turn round, secured Thirlestaine House and began to hack his way out. An omnibus ran twice a week for two years, carrying books from Broadway to Cheltenham. Sir Thomas went on bidding for another thirteen years; then, in 1872, he gave his last nod. The dispersal of the Phillipps Library began in 1886. By 1908 twelve auctions had realized £41,000, in addition to private sales by the executors. Sotheby's periodical auctions of the library have now been going on for sixty-one years. They are not nearly over.

PAINSWICK

Stanley Anderson, R.A.

Almost everything in Painswick is worth a drawing. Besides being one of the most beautiful of the smaller Cotswold towns, it happens, owing to the local freestone of which it is built, to be one of the whitest.

The view here is of Victoria Street. Between the baker's shop on the right and Mr. Watkins's bootshop round the corner on the left, one advances with some eagerness towards the fine mansion with the balustraded roof-line. It turns out to be a tea-shop; and, though it remains a handsome and in no way disfigured building, it administers a slight check. Such adaptations are rare in Painswick.

Behind the houses on the left is the central, and the most commonly pictured, feature of the town—St. Mary's Church. Its tall spire and its magnificent tomb-stones (the work of the Bryans) are, strange to say, apt to be ignored by both guide-book and sightseer in favour of its yew-trees. No fewer than ninety-nine of these trimmed and famous trees flourish in the churchyard. A hundredth, according to local tradition, will not flourish; it has often been planted, and always died.

STANLEY ANDERSON. 1940

KING'S MILL HOUSE, PAINSWICK

Michael Rothenstein

In the Parish Register of 1495 there is mention of Kyngesmill, Agnes Mylls being then the occupier, but a mill-house had probably stood on the site for centuries before that date. According to the late Sir Francis Hyett's careful and instructive little book, *Glimpses of the History of Painswick*, King's Mill was a cloth mill till well into the nineteenth century, being operated by Messrs. Palling, a family of cloth-makers long established in the district. By 1870 the mill had become a pin factory (Messrs. Watkins & Okey); it has also been a flour-mill; to-day it is a private and most desirable residence.

Defoe, travelling through the neighbourhood in 1727, found that 'the Clothiers lye all along the Banks of the River for near 20 Miles'. There were twelve mills on the edge of Painswick itself. Scarlet cloth was the speciality, and the stream ran red with the dye. Defoe saw two pieces of broadcloth being made, 'one Scarlet, the other Crimson in Grain, on purpose to be presented, the one to His Majesty King *George*, and the other to the Prince; when the former was Elector of *Hanover*, and the latter, Electoral Prince.... The Cloth was valued, including the Colour, at 45s. *per* Yard: Indeed it was hardly to be valued, nothing so rich being ever made in *England* before, at least as I was informed.'

The mill-tail still runs beneath the house, serving to provide it with electricity. As for the house itself, it has been adapted, added to, and reshaped for four hundred years. Above the remains of Tudor mullions may be seen the Queen Anne windows put in, no doubt, because they were then 'the thing'. Below the 1850 roof, on the left of the drawing, can be seen the far older accommodation for pigeons, some 40 holes now used by a cosmopolitan crowd of martins, wagtails, and other squatters; and lower still stretches the wall of a long room, now a library but designed and used by the eighteenth-century clothmakers as a workshop. It has a small balcony a few feet from the ground, convenient for tipping rolls of cloth into a cart. The clipped yews in the garden, like a musical allusion to an earlier theme, are a reminder of the churchyard.

Michael Rothenstein 1990.

GATE-HOUSE, FROCESTER COURT

Robert Swan

Frocester Court, near Stroud, sometimes finds its way into the guide-books on the strength of its large tithe barn, a thirteenth-century building standing in the farm-yard and still in good order.

The house itself was built by George Huntley in the reign of Queen Mary. Twenty years later her mobile half-sister, Queen Elizabeth, broke her journey to Berkeley Castle by staying for two nights at Frocester Court. One of those decisions she so hated to make, one of the most important, a finally undodgeable decision, lay just ahead of her. A few months later the desperate but resolute Dutch people offered her their sovereignty in the hope of averting the dominion of papist Spain. She declined, of course; but she promised help.

Though not untouched, though, indeed, showing signs of careful preservation, the gate-house is of the period and may well, as is believed, have been built to com-memorate the royal visit.

HOUSES, STROUD

Walter E. Spradbery

Stroud is a steep place. Its narrow streets are usually full of vehicles anxiously and loudly ascending or descending; and the strange driver, with no leisure to ask the way or heed the instructions, angry or helpful, on the signboards, can do more than ordinary damage. For all these reasons the town is best explored on foot, and only on foot can some of its minor architectural secrets be discovered.

In Nelson Street and elsewhere it is not very difficult to find seventeenth-century houses, like those shown here. Most of them have no history; their faces are their fortune, and both are modest. In many cases they have been occupied, since the day they were built, by makers of the broadcloth from which Stroud has always got its living.

THE MARKET, TETBURY

Louisa Puller

Tetbury stands not far from where the Avon rises, and on the very border of Wiltshire. County delimitations often, indeed usually, pay no respect to local characteristics and love to traverse them; but here in the approach from the east a change in building material forces itself on the attention. The Gloucestershire stone has only just begun by the time one gets to Tetbury.

At the top of the steep hill are the Town Hall, the church of St. Mary Magdalen with its immense steeple, and all the old town's features noted in guide-books and vignetted in the volumes impelled by a walking tour or ramble. The lowly market is generally ignored. It is a busy and businesslike place, serving a large area, and it is picturesquely set against a backcloth of stone buildings, stone walls, and rising roofs. The most numerous, the most noticeable, the oldest pens are for sheep—Tetbury had its wool-market in Elizabethan days—but there are also larger stalls for cattle, on the right. Handy on the left are water and the railway.

BEVERSTONE CASTLE, NEAR TETBURY

Louisa Puller

Beverstone Castle, though always of minor size and importance, and overshadowed by Berkeley, has seen life; and what it has to say is worth listening to.

Since the site commands the Cirencester road and a ford over the river at Anst, it is thought to have been fortified as early as the eleventh century, but mention of a castle does not occur before the thirteenth. When it comes, it has a wonderfully familiar ring, Maurice Fitzharding giving offence to Henry III 'by fortifying his castle at Beverstone without a licence'. Later the Berkeleys, who had been deprived of the lordship of the manor by Henry I, bought it back from the Fitzhardings. It was Thomas, the 3rd Lord Berkeley, who thus regained the family property. His plans received a check when the French, having captured him in the wars of Edward III, paid him the embarrassing compliment of fixing his ransom at a crippling figure. He learned from adversity, and at Poitiers spared so many French lives and showed such appreciation of his prisoners' worth that he recovered his losses with interest and put Beverstone into thorough repair.

It remained in the Berkeleys' possession till 1597, when Sir John, the last of his line, at the last of his resources, sold it to Sir John Poyntz. He resold it to Sir Michael Hicks, and it stayed in the Hicks family until 1842, when it passed to the Holfords. Meanwhile, its appearance was changing no less rapidly than its ownership. After a fire, near the end of the Berkeley tenure, the big banqueting hall was turned into a farm-house. In the course of the fighting in the next century this house, too, was burned down. Colonel Massie, having tried and failed to blow in the great door of the castle, returned in 1644 with cavalry and infantry; and, in the absence of its commander, the garrison surrendered to the Parliamentary forces. The farm-house was again rebuilt in 1691 and, after lasting about a hundred years, once more caught fire. The house then took its present form.

The view here, from the south-east, shows how the farm-house has grown out of the west façade of the castle. In spite of its towers, its moat, and some massive Norman work (with which Maurice Fitzharding can have had nothing to do), Beverstone slipped into the category of castellated mansion or fortified manor; but, as we have seen, it was still a hard nut to crack. Most of these details, and others also, will be found in Sir James Mackenzie's *The Castles of England*.

DOUBLE DOVECOT, COLN ST. ALDWYN

George Bissill

According to the blacksmith who plies his forge just outside the left edge of the drawing, 'double dovecot' is a misnomer. Only one of the twin turrets held pigeons; in the other, hawks were kept. The doves and the falcons used to be raced, he says, against one another.

His first statement may be correct. One of the turrets may have been a mew-house, or moulting house, for hawks; or it may have been used for young hawks during training, when they had to spend longish periods in the dark, or else ensiled (i.e. with eyelids stitched). When their handling and education had proceeded further, they were flown at quarry released at short range—a few yards at first, with the distance gradually increasing. Pigeons, bred for bait as well as for domestic consumption, were useful at this stage. Indeed, the only kind of hawk that the yeoman could afford, the goshawk, cannot even kill a pigeon except at fairly short range. It is thus easy to see how the notion came about that the birds were being raced. But the peregrine can fly at 60 m.p.h. or more, and even if it could be trained to race there would be little excitement and no betting.

In a corner of Williamstrip Park, the yard still serves to house a few farm-carts, but it is falling into decay and disrepair. Even so, it is at least 3,500 years younger than the sport of falconry. In England hawking has been on the decline since the days of Charles II, when the sporting gun made its appearance and certain birds began to be categorized as 'game'. Yet it has never died out. Hawks are still trained and kept, and flown at grouse, black game, partridges, pheasants, quail, landrails, duck, teal, woodcock, snipe, hares, and rabbits. The woodcock is their especial favourite, and will persuade even the feeblest falcon, it is said, to put its best pinion forward.

THE PARAGON, CLIFTON

Phyllis Ginger

In 1785 Clifton, like Buxton, seems to have decided to have a cut at Bath; and from the cliff on which it stands terraces and crescents spilled over into the gorge of the Avon. The period was good, the effects are happy, but optimism and ill luck brought, at the time, disaster. The long French wars began, and no fewer than 500 houses were left unfinished and often roofless. The Royal York Crescent, queening it high above its neighbours, was twenty-seven years in building and had a narrow escape, in its rough state, of being requisitioned as a barracks. For other areas James Wyatt was retained. Fortunately for the speculators, if unfortunately for us, there was time to cancel his engagement.

The name of the architect of The Paragon is lost; but, whoever he was, he managed to get his curving cul-de-sac built in 1809 or 1810—a charming retreat of sixteen houses, all (except Nos. 1, 2, and 16) beautifully harmonious and complete with semicircular porch and convex double doors. At the back, above cellars or coach-houses, runs a balustraded terrace common to the residents and giving access to a precipitous garden; and from the terrace, from the iron verandas at the first floor, and still better from the top windows a superb view embraces, low and distant, the funnels and cranes of the port of Bristol.

There was a time when, for half a mile round The Paragon, the paving-stones echoed more often to the feet of the famous than, perhaps, any equivalent stretch outside London, Bath, and Newmarket. No general list can be even attempted; but a sub-list, of literary ladies who (just before, after, or during the construction of The Paragon) could be met there, may be of interest. At 36 Royal York Crescent, behind our left shoulder as we look at the picture, Mrs. Thrale spent the last months of her life. Not far off Lady Hesketh had been living when, to a letter of hers describing the scene, Cowper roused himself, almost for the last time, to pen a reply. Hannah More resided at 4 Windsor Terrace; and at 15 Vyvyan Terrace those other and even dimmer schoolmistresses, Harriet and Sophia Lee, had their seminary. One of their *Canterbury Tales* (Harriet's *Kruitzner*) made a lasting impression on Byron, and was the basis of his *Werner*. Maria Edgeworth stayed at 14 Prince's Buildings, up the steps on the right; her sister Anna, marrying Dr. Beddoes of 3 Rodney Place, became the mother of Thomas Lovell Beddoes. But of all the descriptions of the spa, surely the liveliest is to be found in *Evelina*, although Fanny Burney seems to have been there for a few hours only.

PRINTED IN GREAT BRITAIN
AT THE UNIVERSITY PRESS, OXFORD
BY CHARLES BATEY
PRINTER TO THE UNIVERSITY